RECORDED VERSIONS GUITAR

AUTHENTIC TRANSCRIPTIONS WITH NOTES AND TABLATURE

IRON MAIDEN
ANTHOLOGY

P9-AQU-433

2	Aces High
11	Be Quick or Be Dead
22	Bring Your Daughter to the Slaughter
35	Can I Play With Madness
45	Evil That Men Do
60	Flight of Icarus
69	Killers
84	No Prayer for the Dying
97	The Number of the Beast
108	The Phantom of the Opera
126	Revelations
135	Run to the Hills
144	Running Free
150	The Trooper
161	Two Minutes to Midnight
175	Wasted Years
184	Wrathchild

Cover photo by Ross Halfin/Idols

Music transcriptions by Addi Booth and Paul Pappas

ISBN 0-634-06690-0

HAL•LEONARD®
CORPORATION

7777 W. BLUEMOUND RD. P.O. BOX 13819 MILWAUKEE, WI 53213

For all works contained herein:
Unauthorized copying, arranging, adapting, recording or public performance is an infringement of copyright.
Infringers are liable under the law.

Visit Hal Leonard Online at
www.halleonard.com

Aces High

Words and Music by Steven Harris

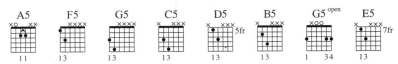

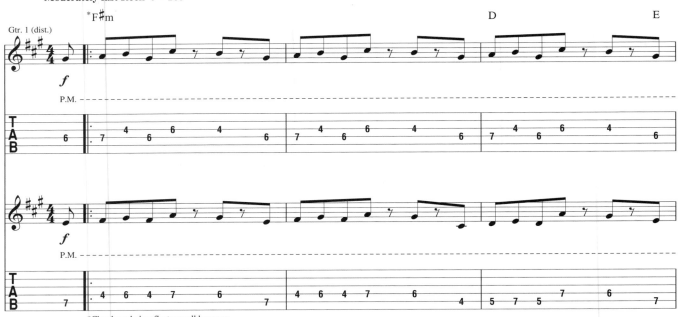

*Chord symbols reflect overall harmony.

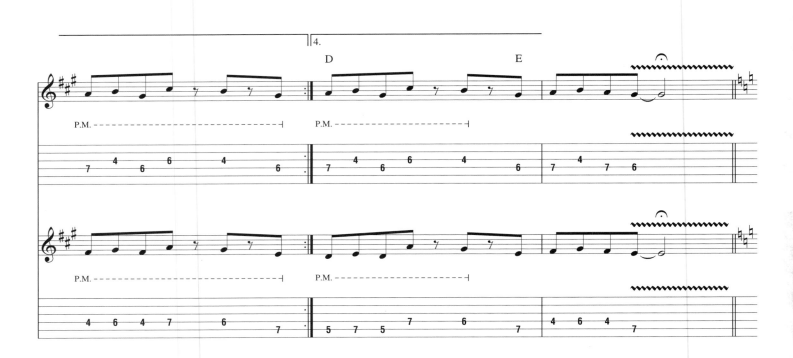

Copyright © 1984 by Iron Maiden Holdings Ltd.
All Rights in the world Administered by Zomba Music Publishers Ltd.
All Rights in the United States and Canada Administered by Zomba Enterprises, Inc.
International Copyright Secured   All Rights Reserved

Faster ♩ = 252

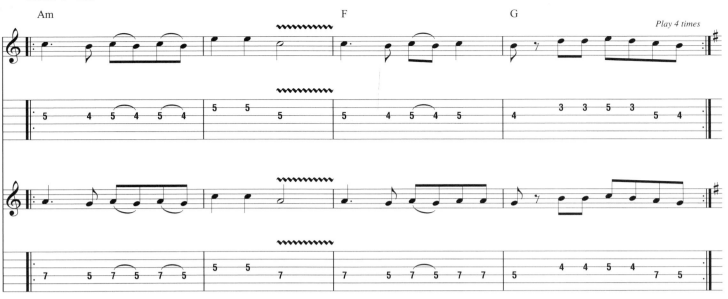

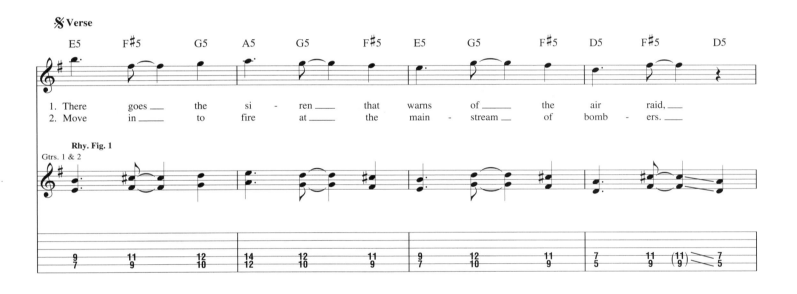

1. There goes the si - ren that warns of the air raid,
2. Move in to fire at the main - stream of bomb - ers.

Rhy. Fig. 1
Gtrs. 1 & 2

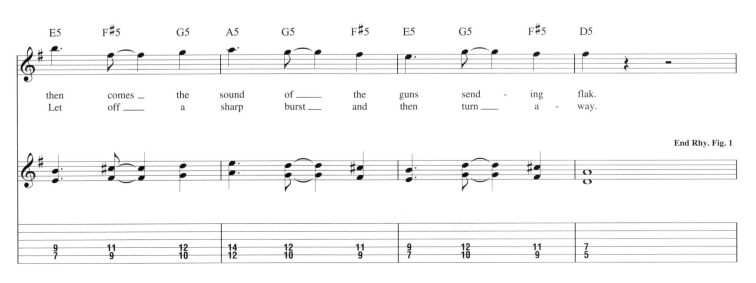

then comes the sound of the guns send - ing flak.
Let off a sharp burst and then turn a - way.

End Rhy. Fig. 1

3

got - ta _____ get air - borne _____ be - fore it's _____ too late.
head - ing _____ straight for them _____ I press down _____ my guns.

Pre-Chorus

1., 2. Run - nin' scramb - lin', fly - in',
3., 4. Roll - in', turn - in', div - in',

Gtr. 1

Gtr. 2

*w/ echo set for half-note regeneration w/ 1 repeat, next 7 meas.

Roll - in', turn - in', div - in'. Go - ing in a - gain.

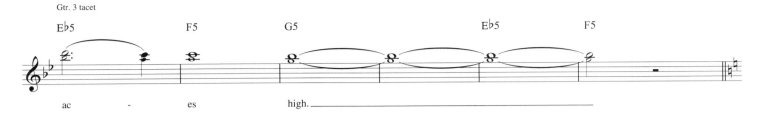

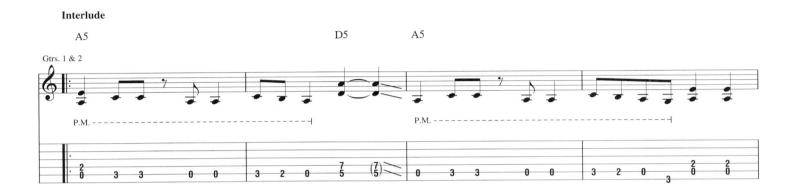

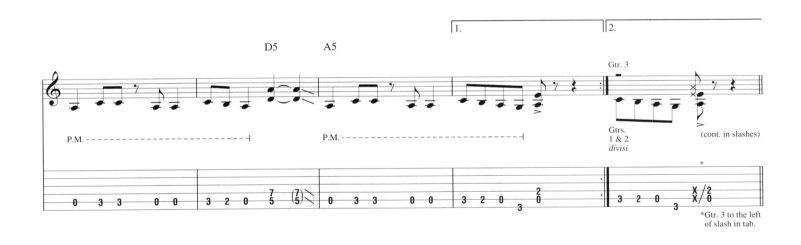

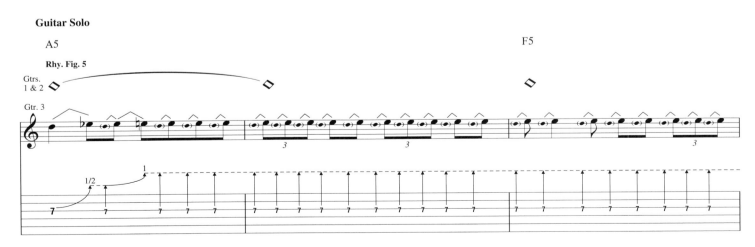

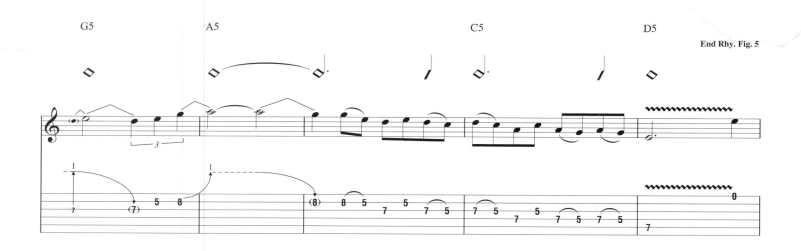

Gtrs. 1 & 2: w/ Rhy. Fig. 5

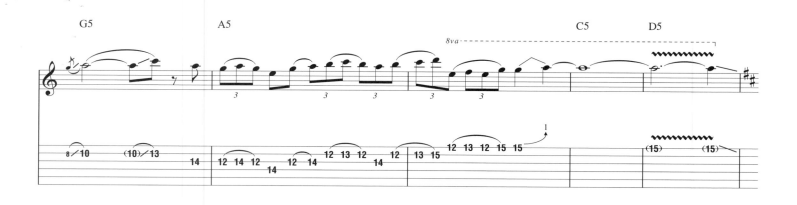

Gtr. 3 tacet

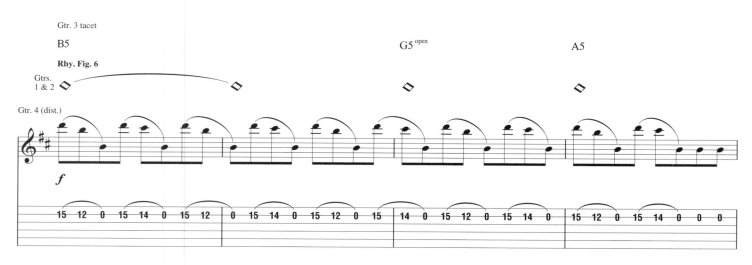

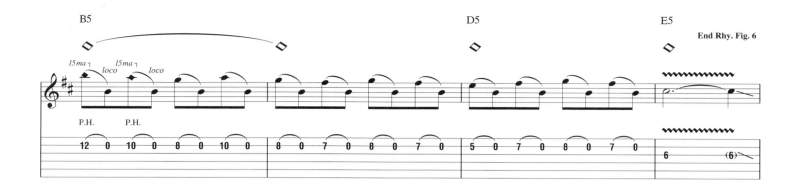

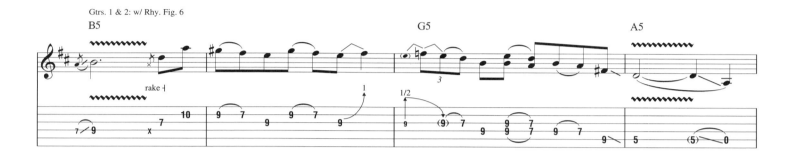

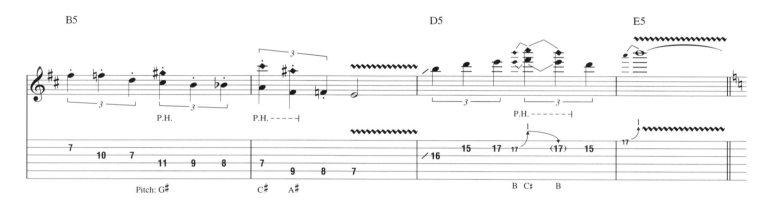

Interlude

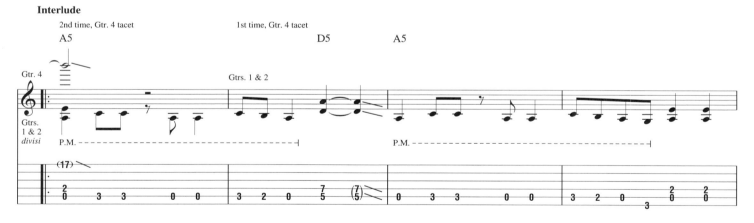

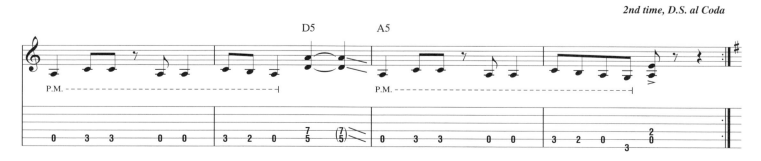

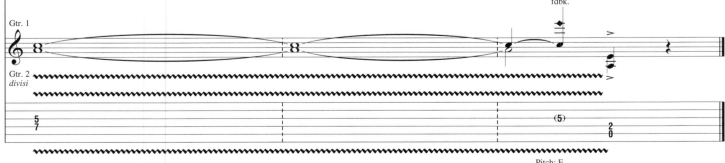

Be Quick or Be Dead

Words and Music by Bruce Dickinson and Janick Gers

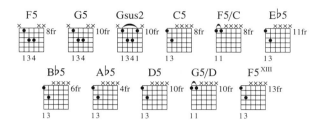

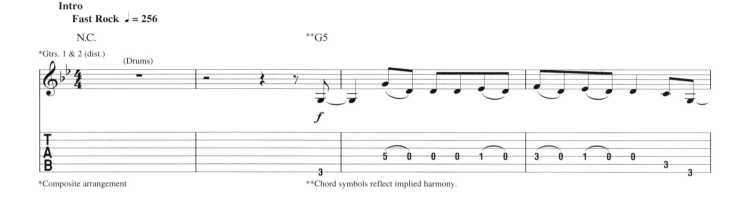

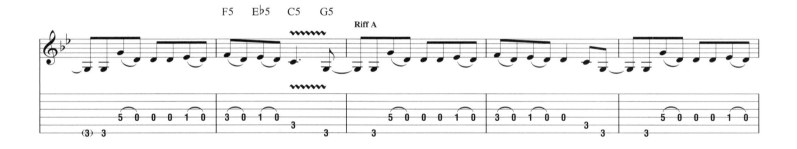

*Composite arrangement

**Chord symbols reflect implied harmony.

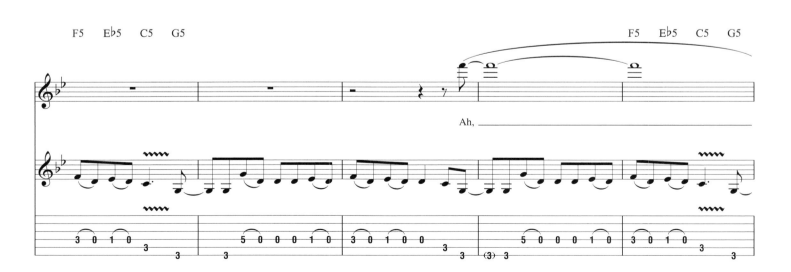

Copyright © 1992 by Iron Maiden Holdings Ltd.
All Rights in the world Administered by Zomba Music Publishers Ltd.
All Rights in the United States and Canada Administered by Zomba Enterprises, Inc.
International Copyright Secured   All Rights Reserved

Gtrs. 1 & 2: w/ Rhy. Fig. 1

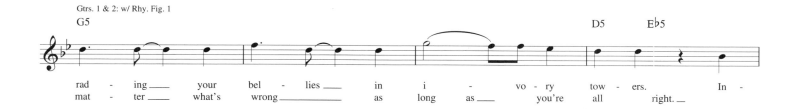

rad - ing ___ your bel - lies ___ in i - vo - ry tow - ers. In -
mat - ter ___ what's wrong ___ as long as ___ you're all right. ___

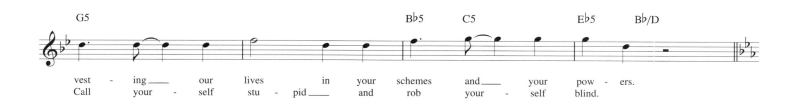

vest - ing ___ our lives in your schemes and ___ your pow - ers.
Call your - self stu - pid ___ and rob your - self blind.

𝄋 𝄋 Pre-Chorus

3rd time, Gtr. 4: w/ Fill 2

You've got to watch them, ___ be quick or ___ be dead. ___

Rhy. Fig. 2

Gtrs. 1 & 2

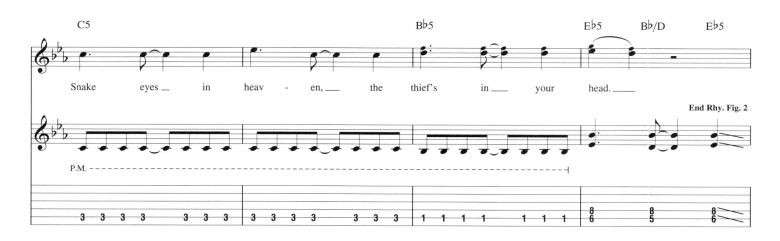

Snake eyes ___ in heav - en, ___ the thief's in ___ your head. ___

End Rhy. Fig. 2

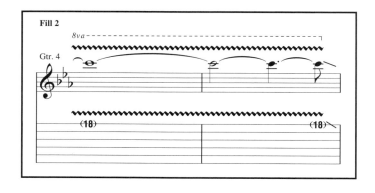

Fill 2

Gtr. 4

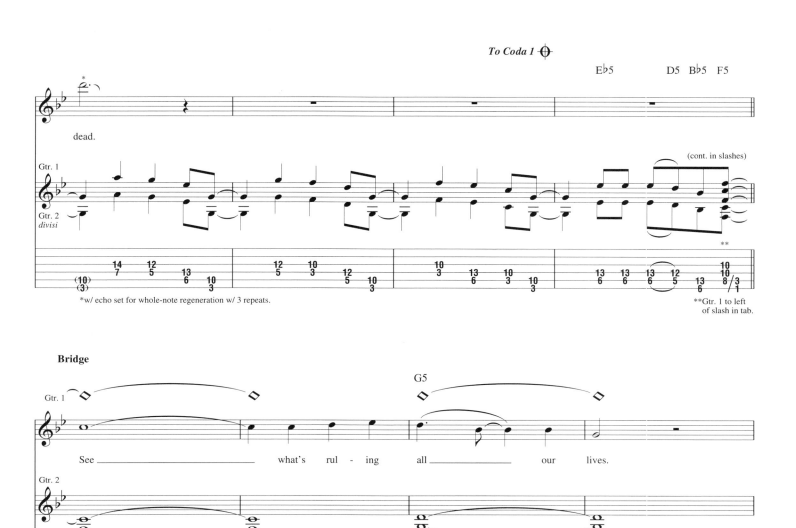

*w/ echo set for whole-note regeneration w/ 3 repeats.

**Gtr. 1 to left of slash in tab.

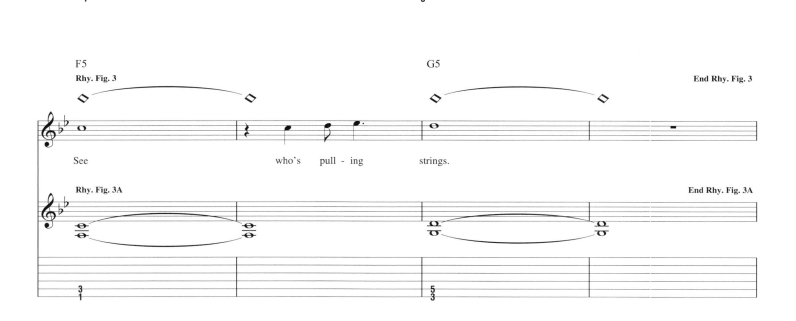

Bridge

See _____ what's rul-ing all _____ our lives.

See who's pull-ing strings.

See what's rul-ing all _____ our lives.

Interlude

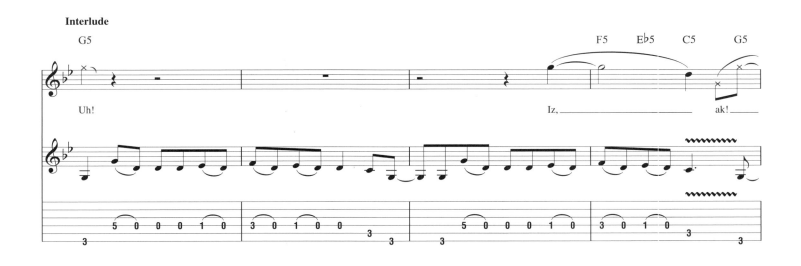

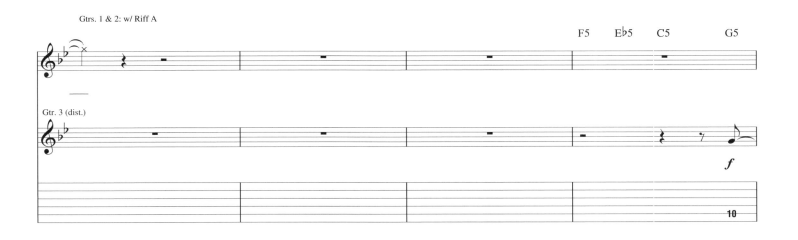

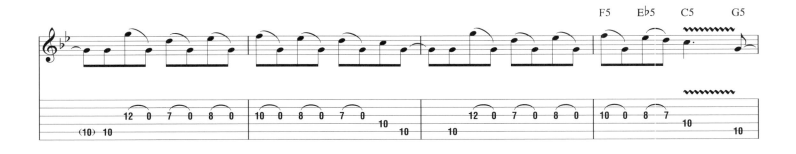

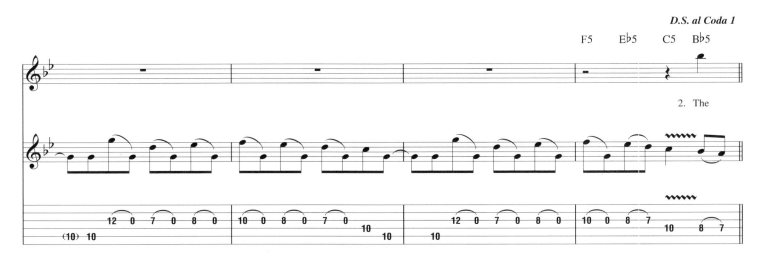

17

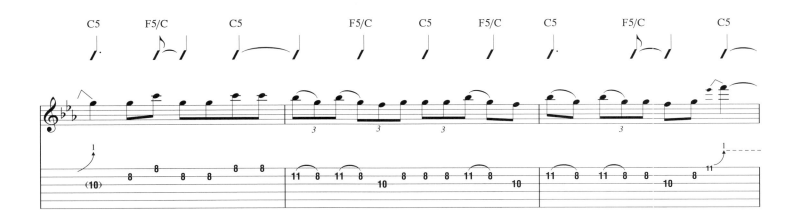

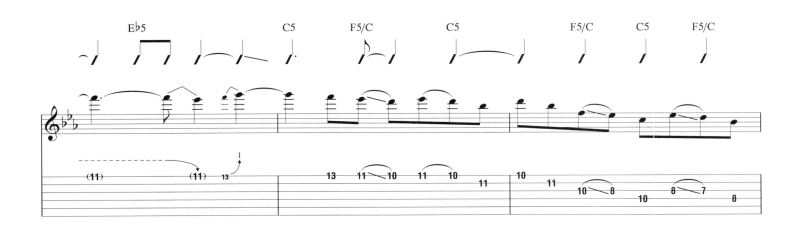

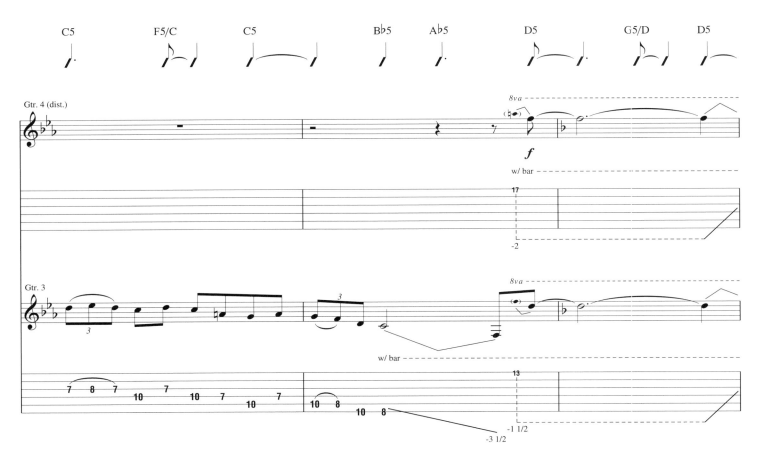

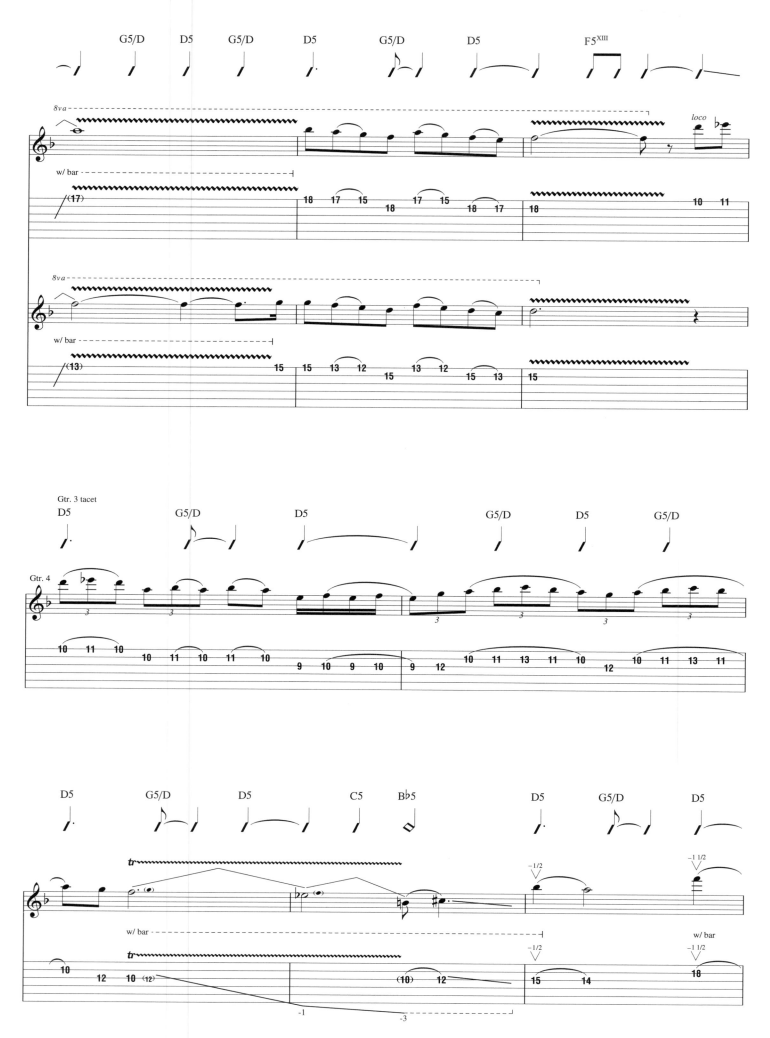

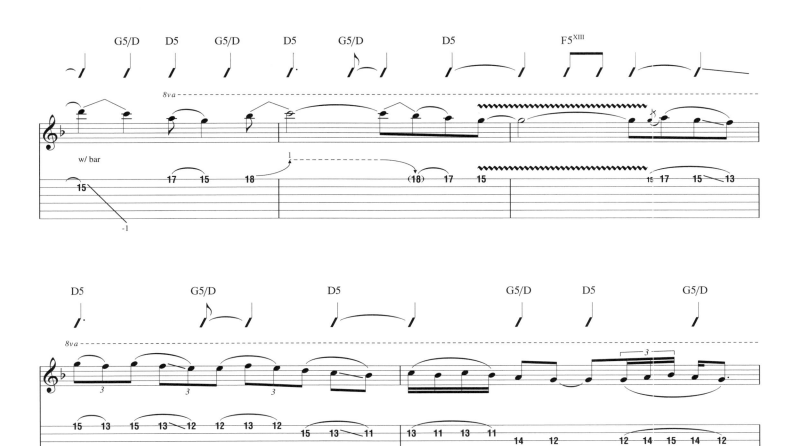

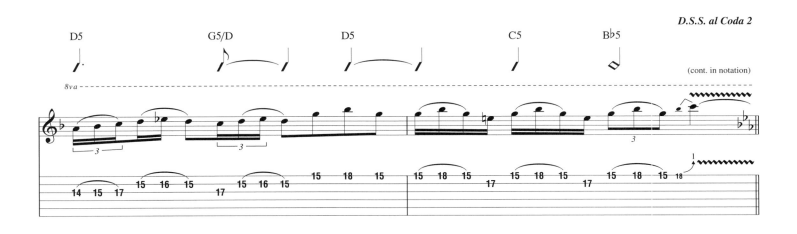

D.S.S. al Coda 2

(cont. in notation)

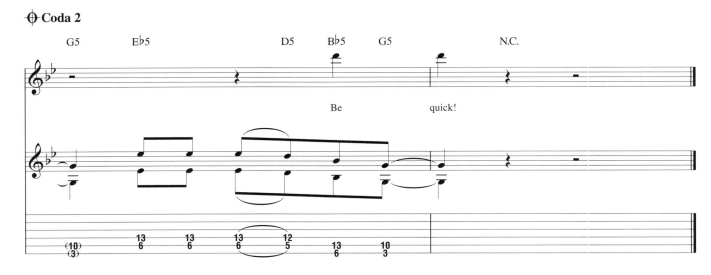

$\oplus$ **Coda 2**

Be   quick!

from *No Prayer for the Dying*

Bring Your Daughter to the Slaughter

Words and Music by Bruce Dickinson

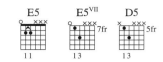

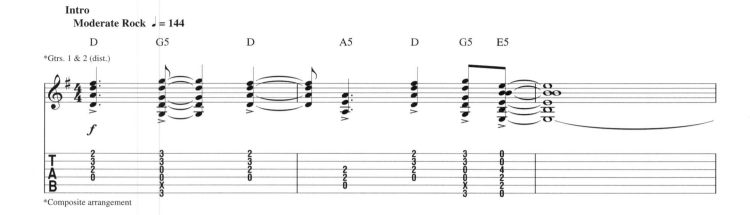

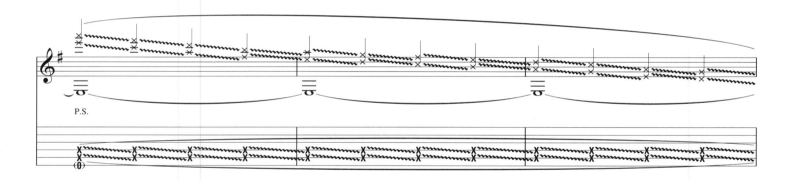

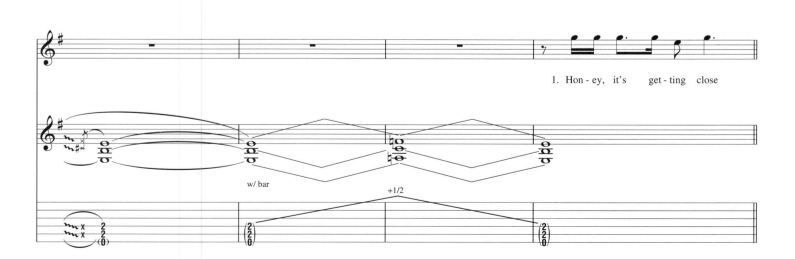

1. Hon - ey, it's get - ting close

Copyright © 1989 by Iron Maiden Holdings Ltd.
All Rights in the world Administered by Zomba Music Publishers Ltd.
All Rights in the United States and Canada Administered by Zomba Enterprises, Inc.
International Copyright Secured   All Rights Reserved

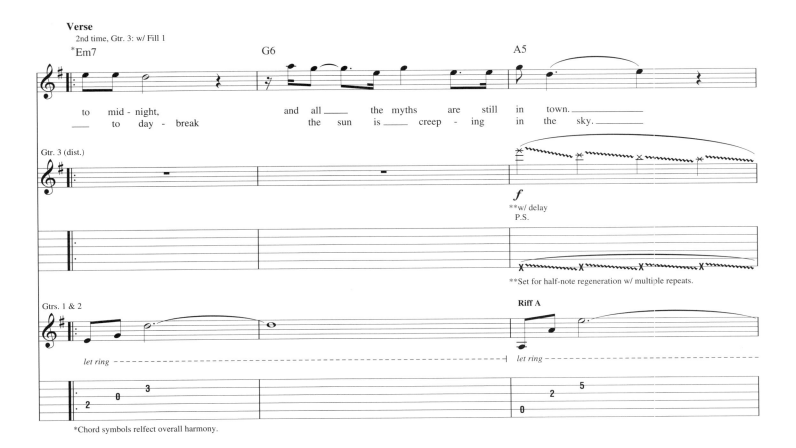

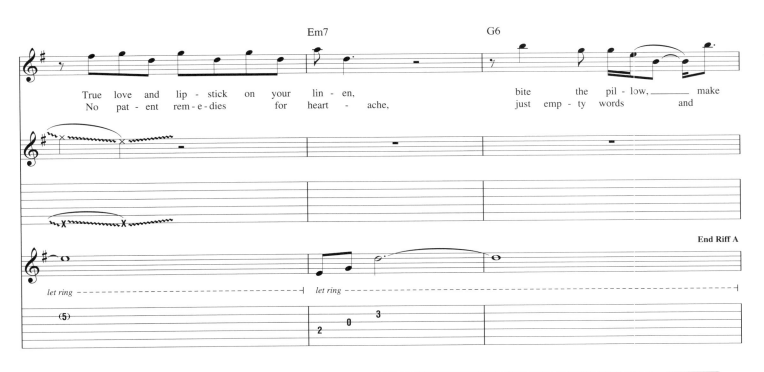

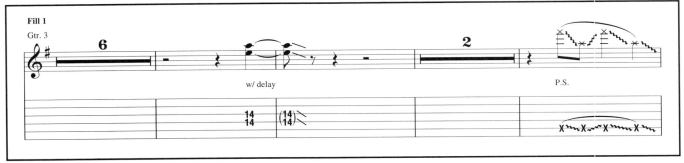

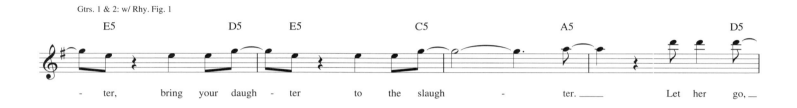

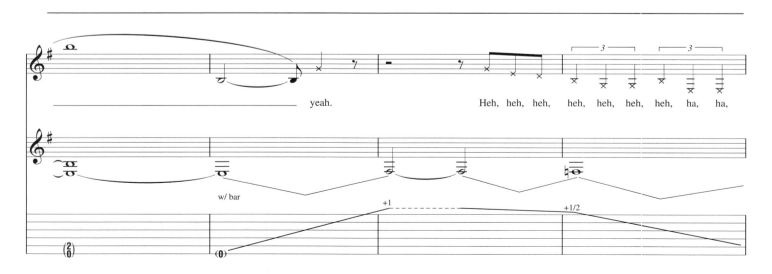

ha.

2. Hon - ey, it's get - ting close

Bridge

N.C.   G5   D

So pick up your fool - ish pride. No go - ing back, no -

G5   D   A5   D   G5   E5

where, no way, no place to hide. Let her go!

Gtr. 4 (dist.)

_f_

Harm.

Pitch: G   w/ bar   -2 1/2

Gtrs. 1 & 2

P.S.

Guitar Solo

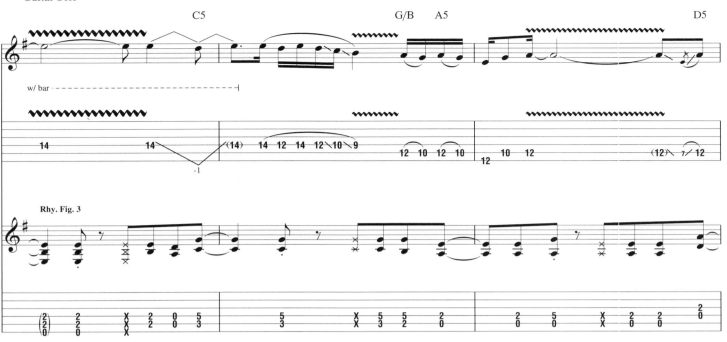

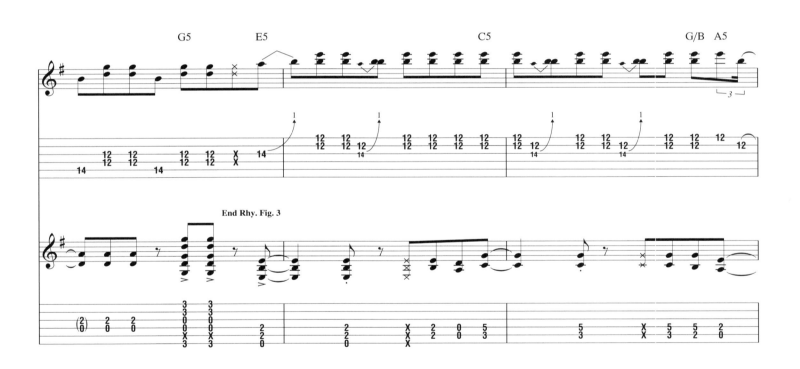

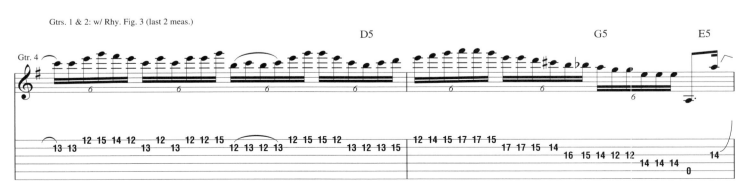

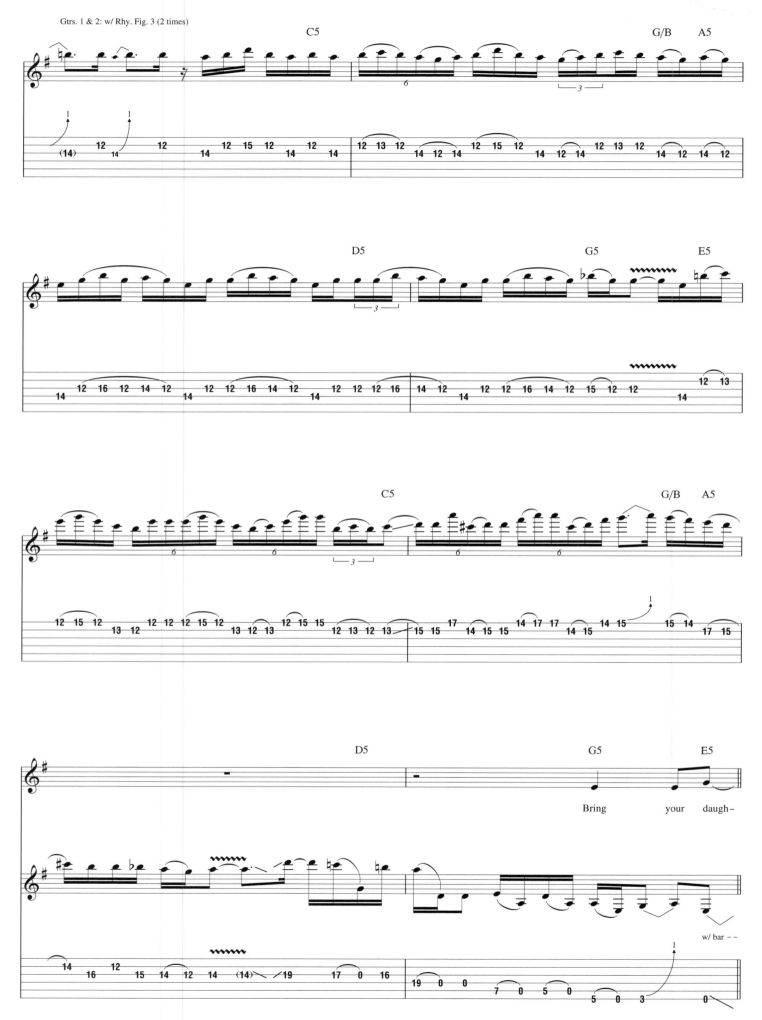

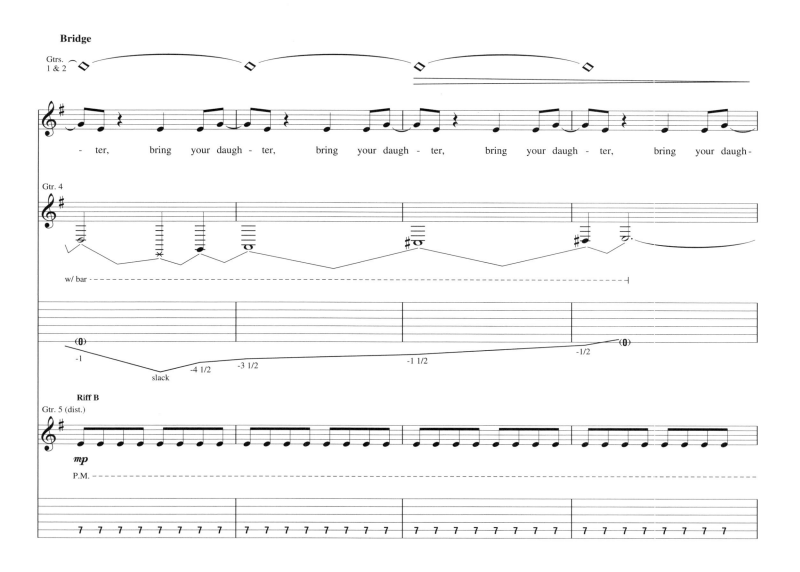

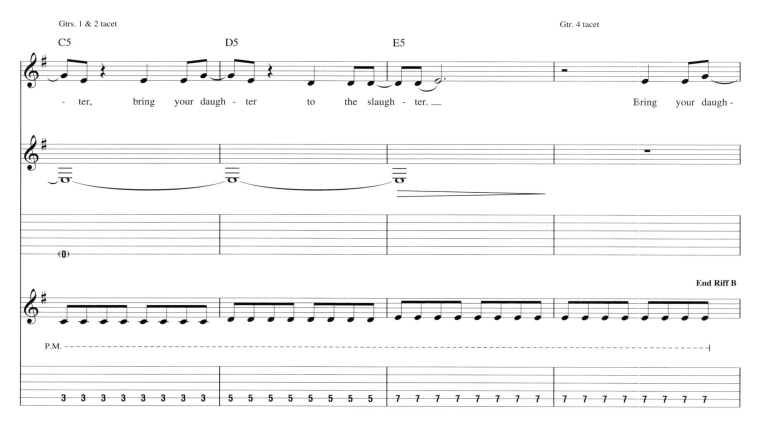

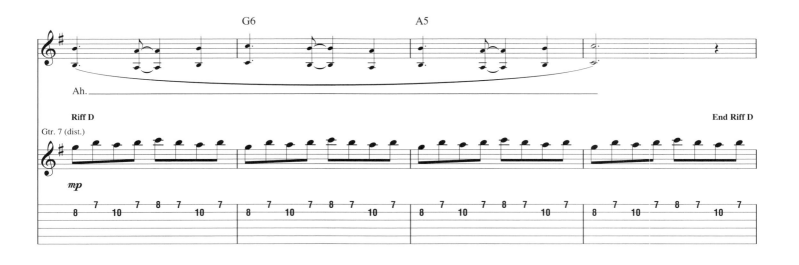

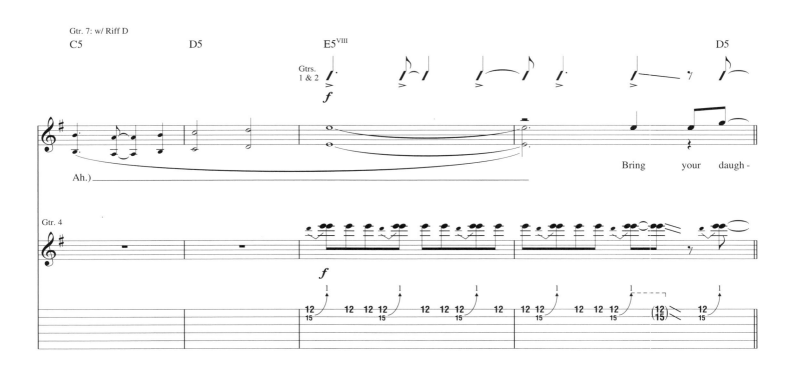

Outro-Chorus

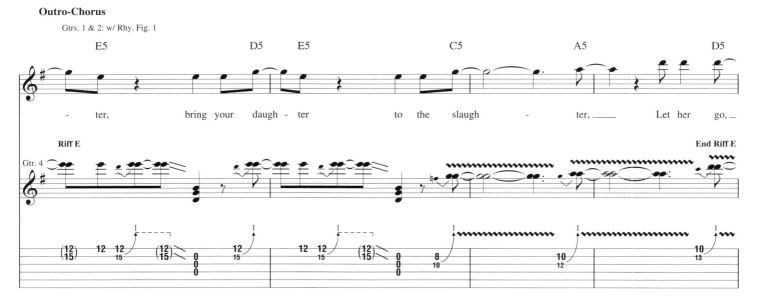

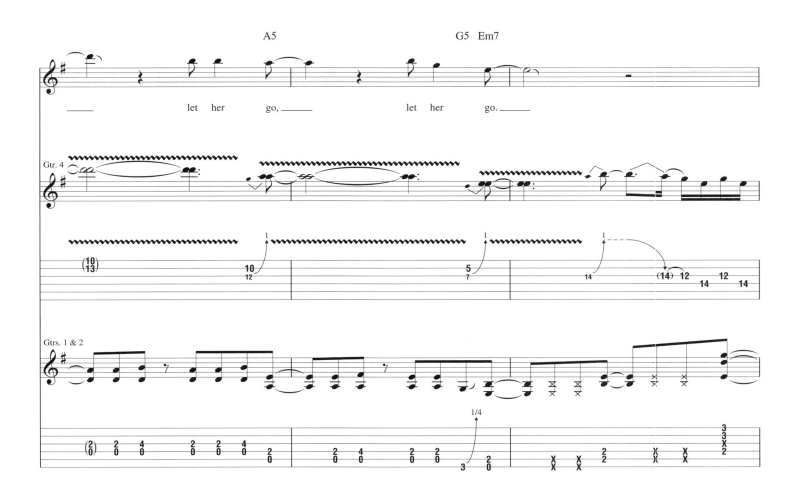

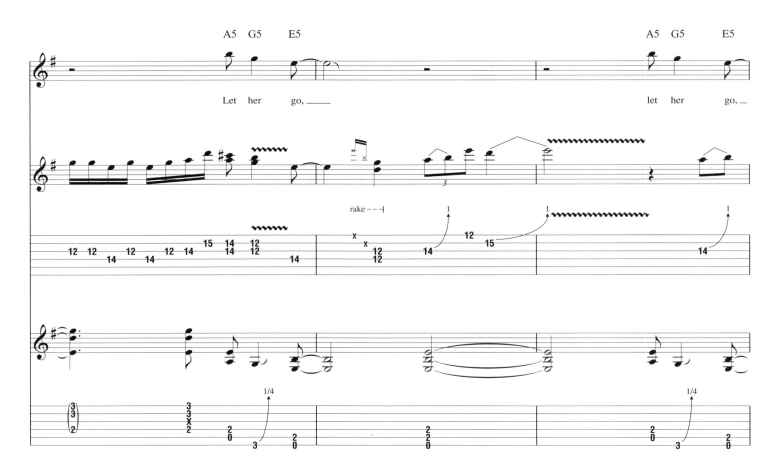

Can I Play With Madness

Words and Music by Bruce Dickinson, Steven Harris and Adrian Smith

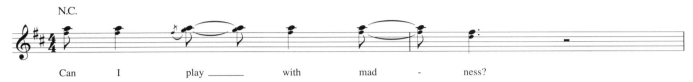

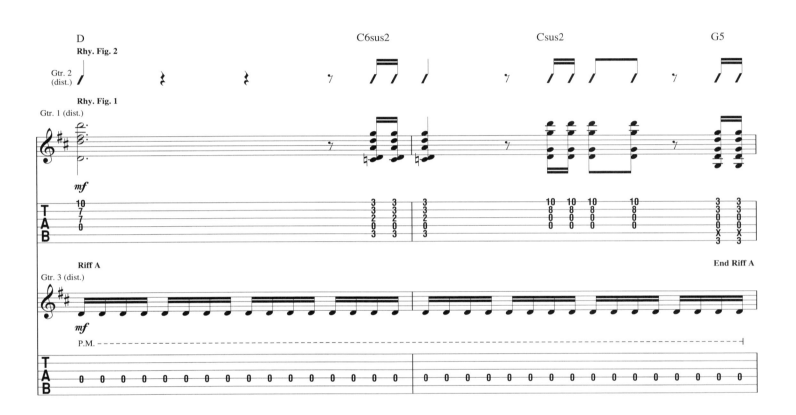

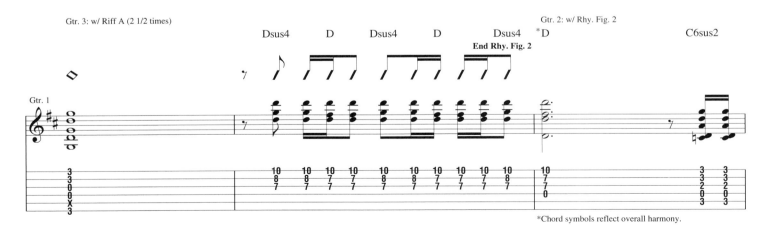

*Chord symbols reflect overall harmony.

Copyright © 1988 by Iron Maiden Holdings Ltd.
All Rights in the world Administered by Zomba Music Publishers Ltd.
All Rights in the United States and Canada Administered by Zomba Enterprises, Inc.
International Copyright Secured   All Rights Reserved

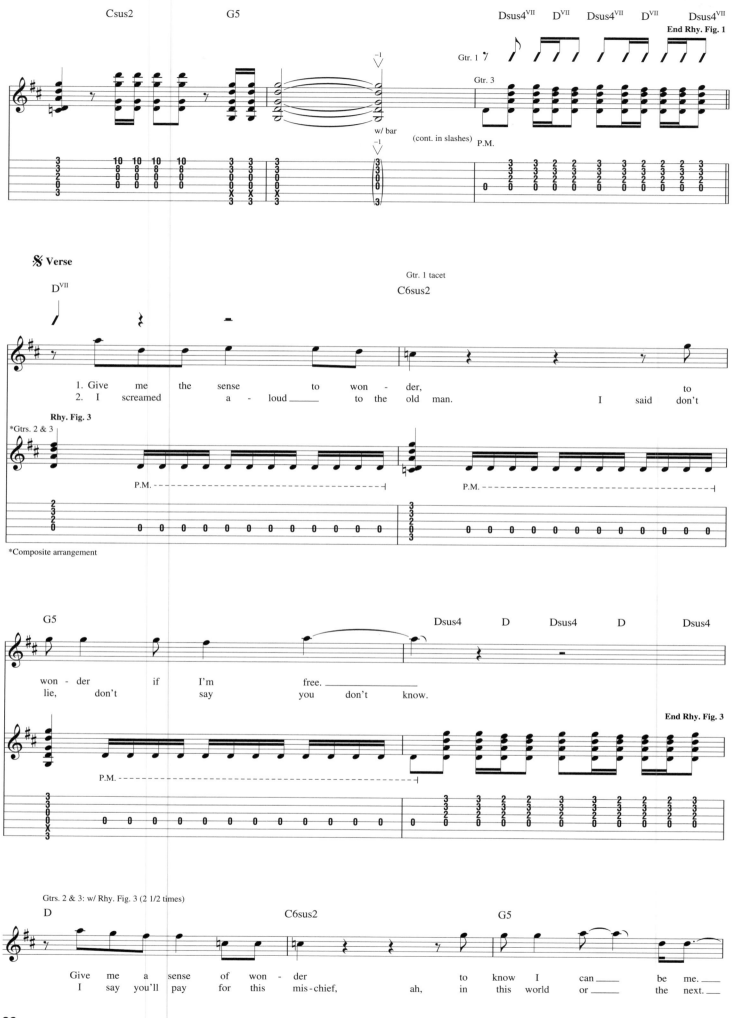

Give me the strength to hold my head up,
Oh, then he fixed me with a freez - ing glance ___ and the

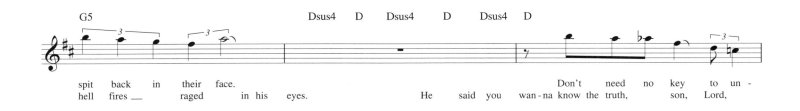

spit back in their face.
hell fires ___ raged in his eyes.
Don't need no key to un -
He said you wan-na know the truth, son, Lord,

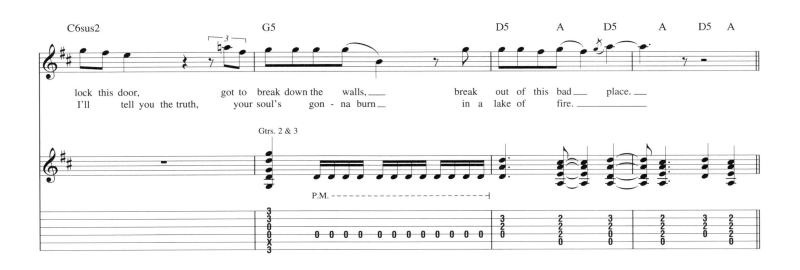

lock this door, got to break down the walls, ___ break out of this bad ___ place. ___
I'll tell you the truth, your soul's gon - na burn ___ in a lake of fire. _____

Chorus

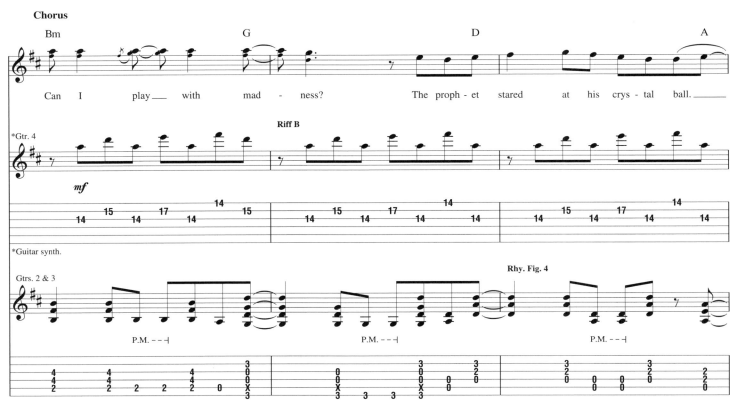

Can I play ___ with mad - ness? The proph - et stared at his crys - tal ball. _____

*Gtr. 4

*Guitar synth.

Gtrs. 2 & 3

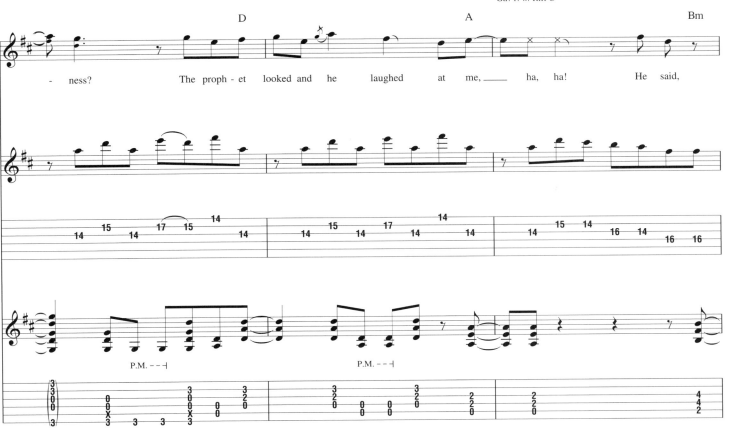

-ness?   The proph-et   looked   and   he   laughed   at   me, ___   ha,   ha!   He   said,

To Coda ⊕

Gtr. 4 tacet

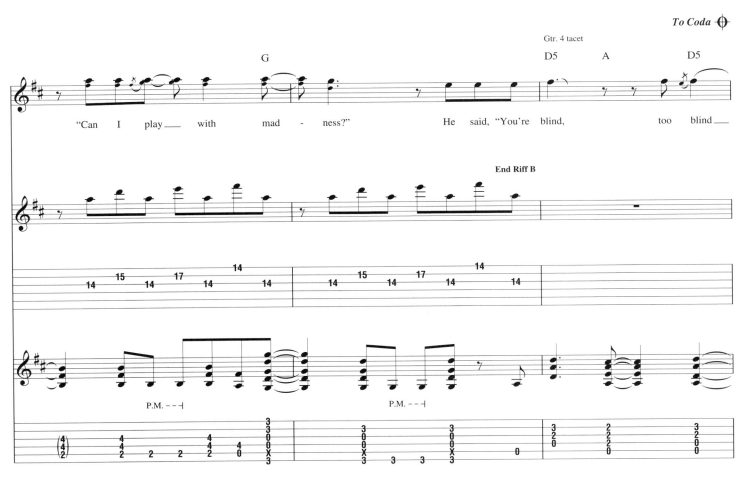

"Can   I   play ___   with   mad-ness?"   He   said,   "You're   blind,   too   blind ___

End Riff B

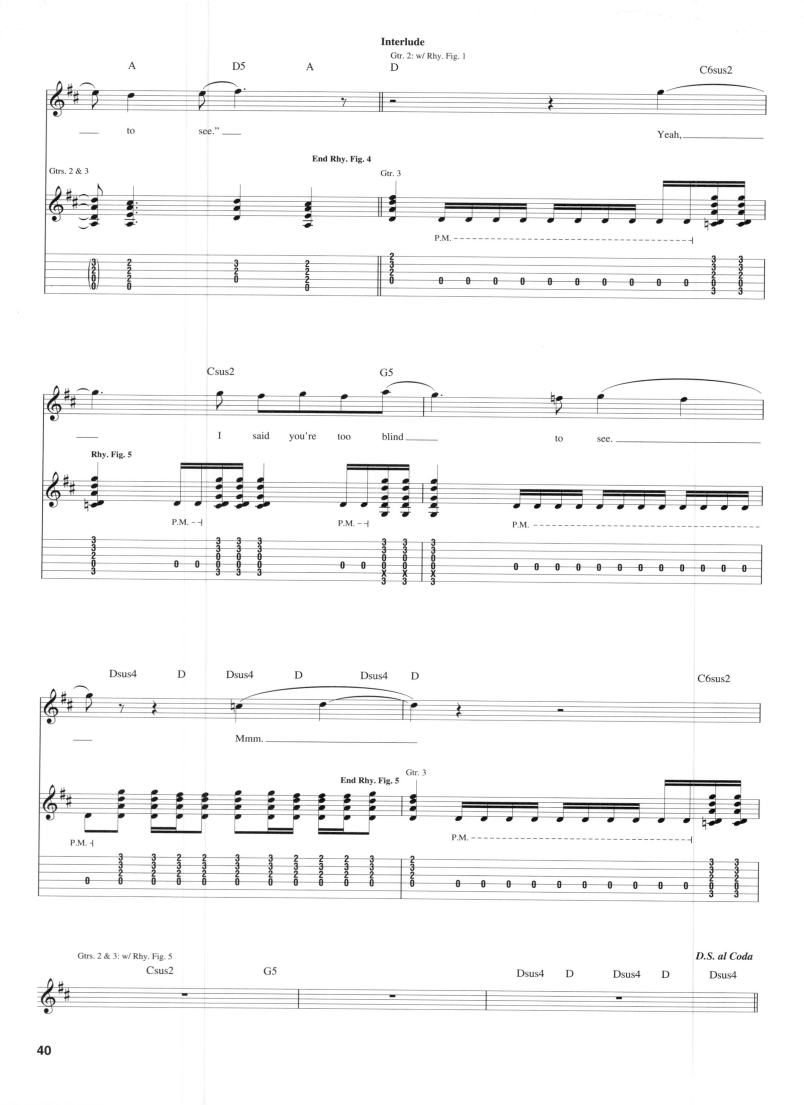

$\oplus$ **Coda**

*Composite arrangement

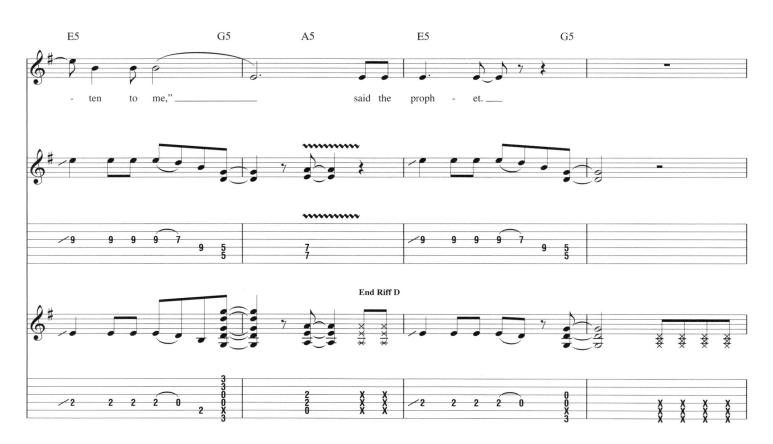

End half-time feel

Guitar Solo

Gtr. 1 tacet
Gtrs. 2 & 3: w/ Riff D (2 times)

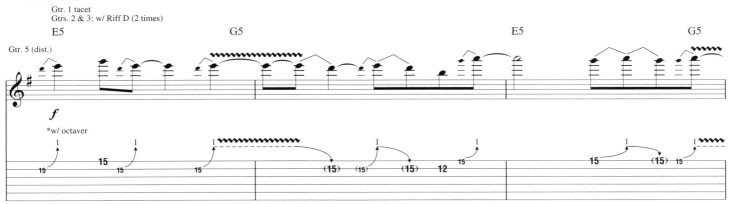

*Set for one octave below.

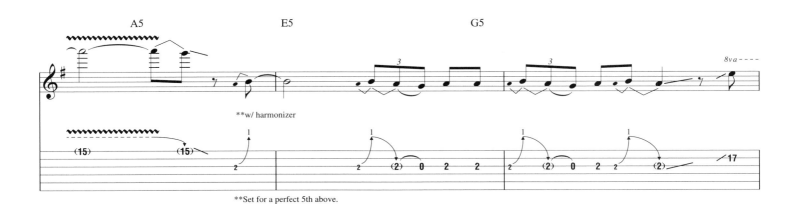

**Set for a perfect 5th above.

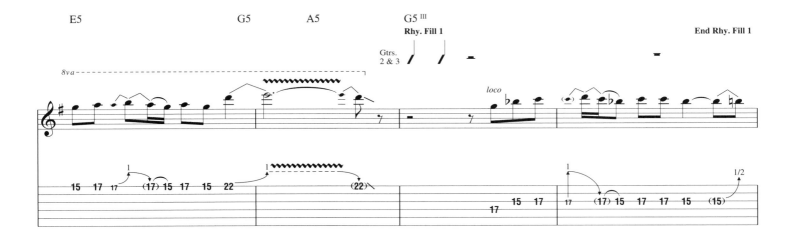

Gtrs. 2 & 3: w/ Rhy. Fill 1 (2 times)

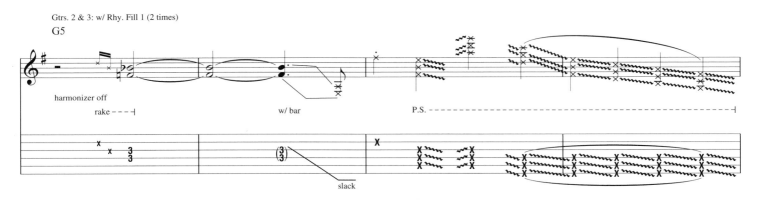

Evil That Men Do

Words and Music by Bruce Dickinson, Steven Harris and Adrian Smith

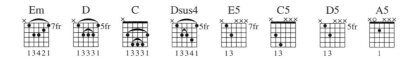

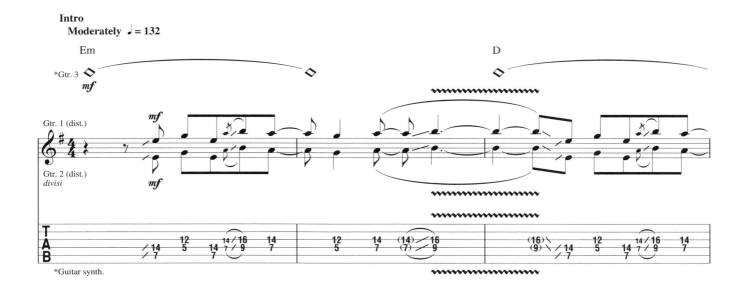

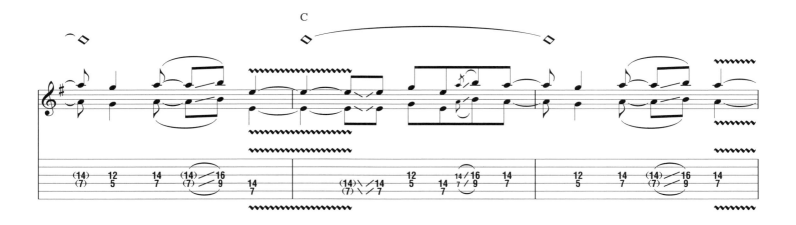

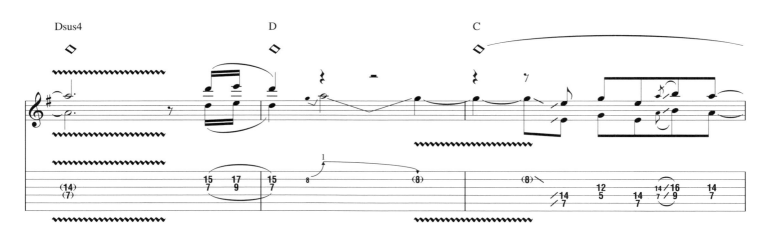

Copyright © 1988 by Iron Maiden Holdings Ltd.
All Rights in the world Administered by Zomba Music Publishers Ltd.
All Rights in the United States and Canada Administered by Zomba Enterprises, Inc.
International Copyright Secured   All Rights Reserved

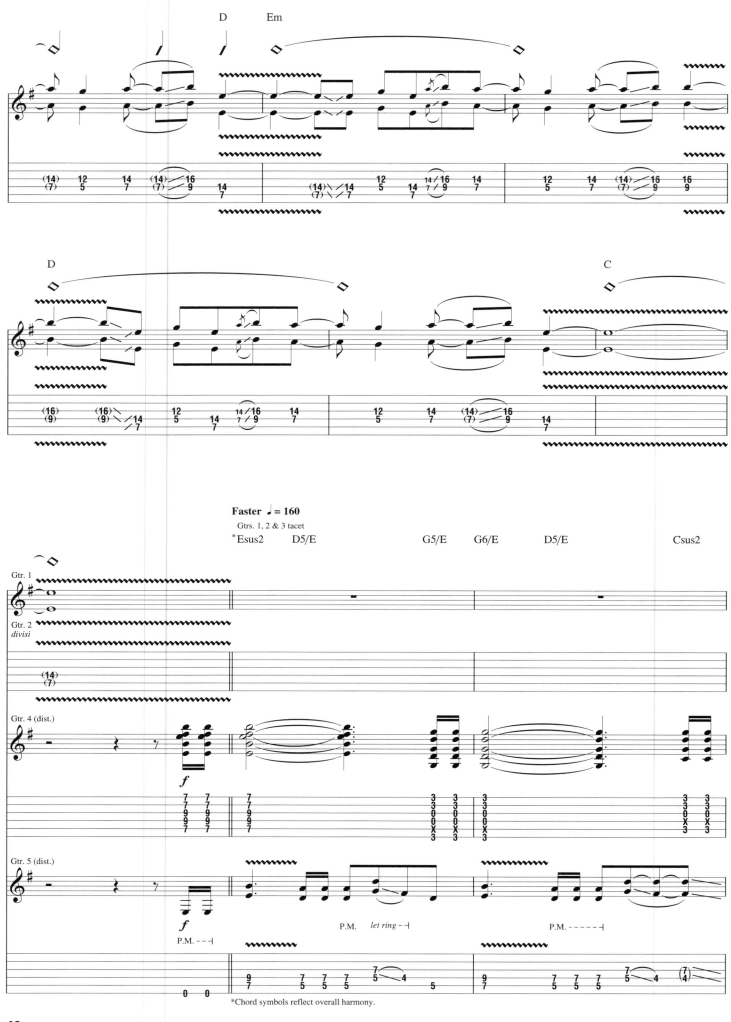

*Chord symbols reflect overall harmony.

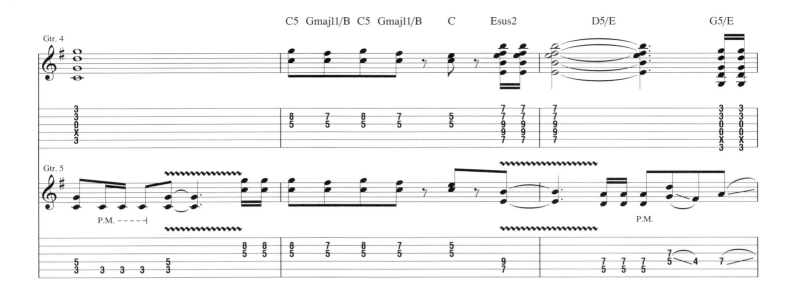

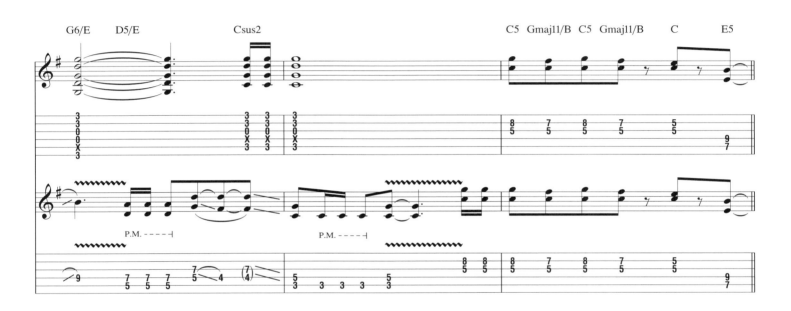

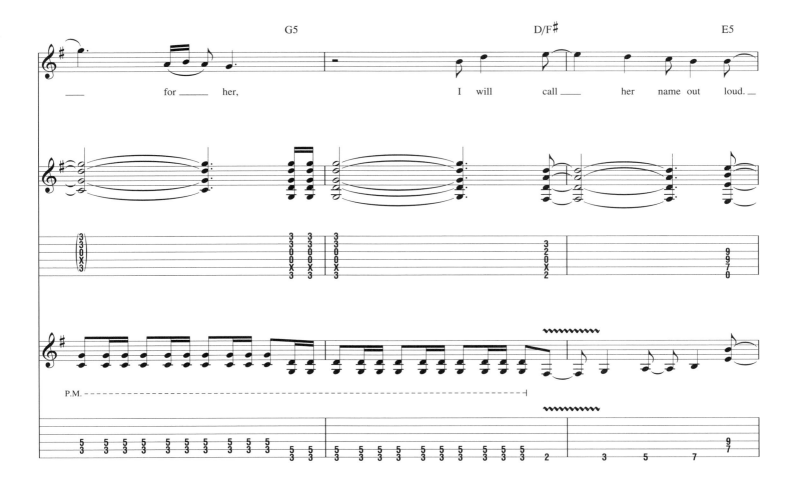

for _____ her, I will call _____ her name out loud. _____

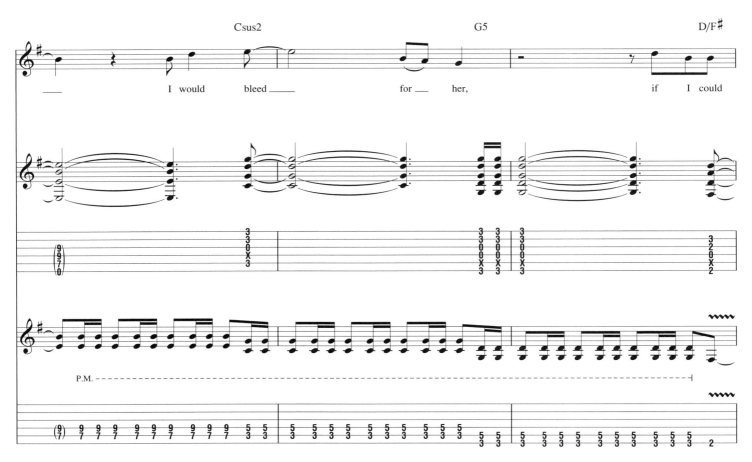

I would bleed _____ for _____ her, if I could

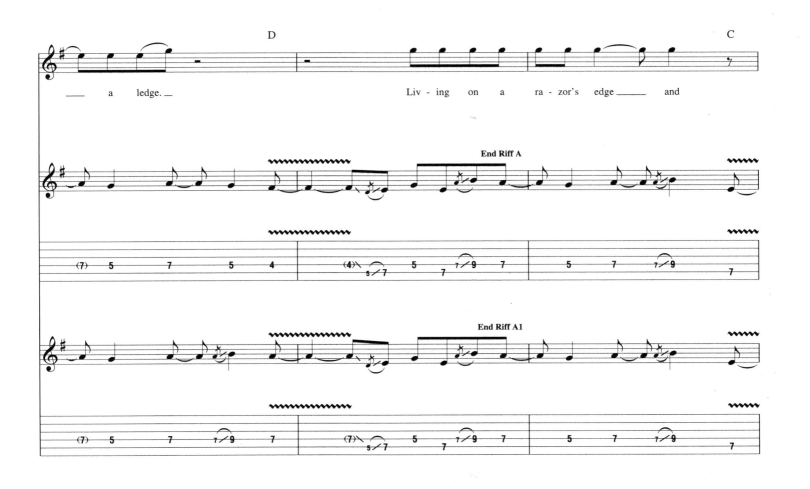

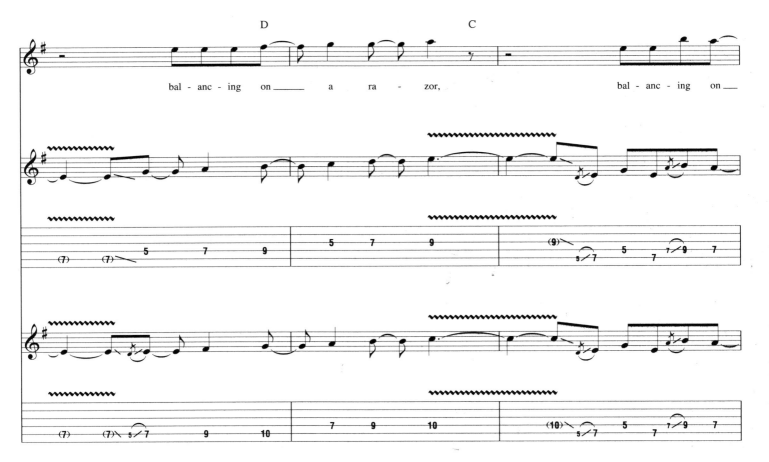

Chorus

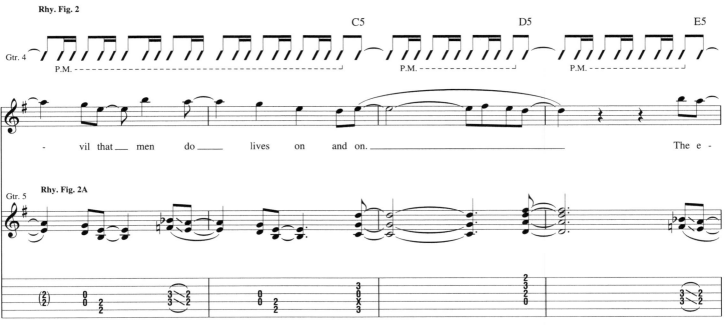

- vil that ___ men do ___ lives on and on. ___ The e -

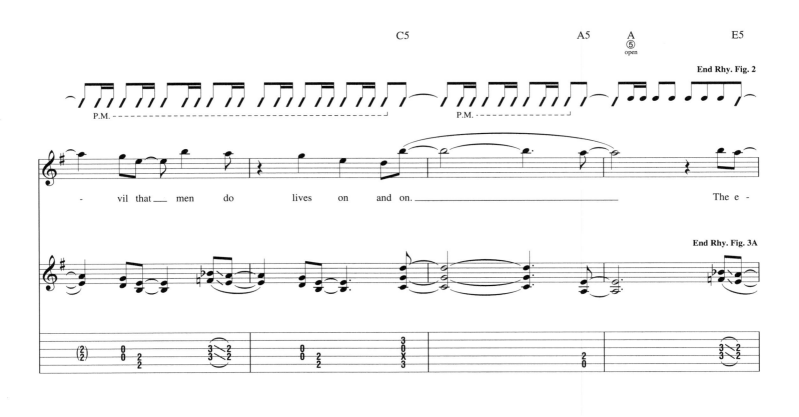

- vil that ___ men do lives on and on. ___ The e -

Gtr. 4: w/ Rhy. Fig. 2
Gtr. 5: w/ Rhy. Fig. 2A (1st 4 meas.)

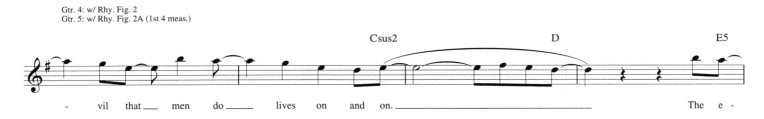

- vil that ___ men do ___ lives on and on. ___ The e -

%8 Pre-Chorus

Gtrs. 4 & 5: w/ Riffs A & A1
2nd time, Gtrs. 1 & 2: w/ Fill 1

Liv- ing on a ra - zor's edge, bal - anc- ing on ____ a ledge. Liv- ing on a

Chorus

Gtrs. 4 & 5: w/ Riffs B & B1

Gtr. 4: w/ Rhy. Fig. 2 (1 7/8 times)
Gtr. 5: w/ Rhy. Fig. 2A (1 3/8 times)

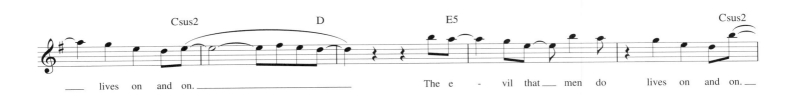

ra - zor's edge. You know, ____ you know ____ the e - vil that ____ men do ____

____ lives on and on. ____ The e - vil that ____ men do lives on and on. ____

The e - vil that ____ men do ____ lives on and on. ____

To Coda ⊕

____ The e - vil that ____ men do lives on and on. ____

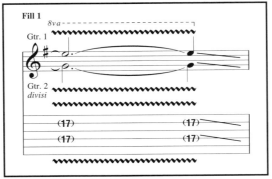

Fill 1

55

Interlude

Guitar Solo

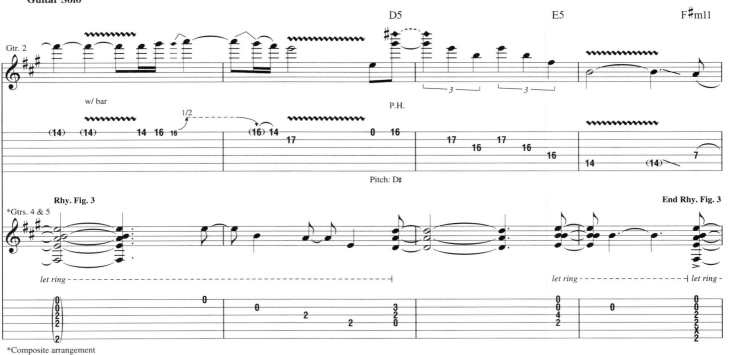

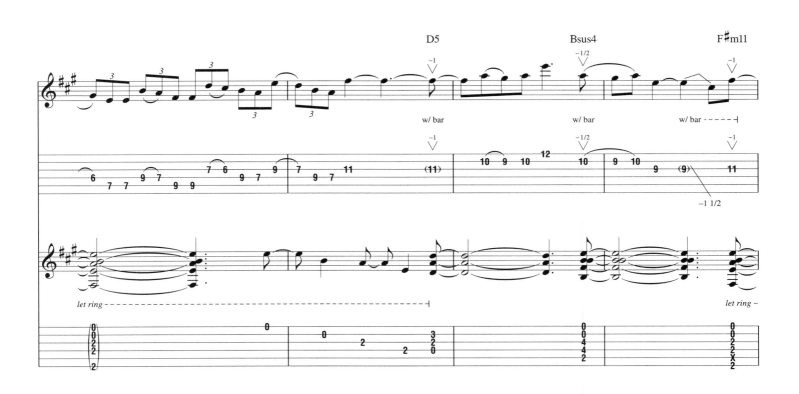

*Composite arrangement

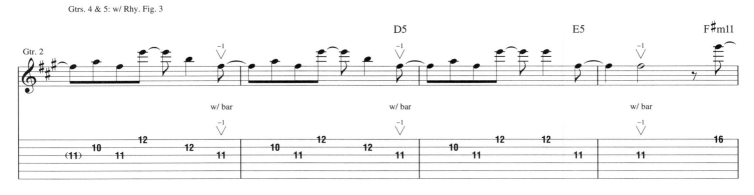

Flight of Icarus

Words and Music by Bruce Dickinson and Adrian Smith

Copyright © 1983 by Iron Maiden Holdings Ltd.
All Rights in the world Administered by Zomba Music Publishers Ltd.
All Rights in the United States and Canada Administered by Zomba Enterprises, Inc.
International Copyright Secured   All Rights Reserved

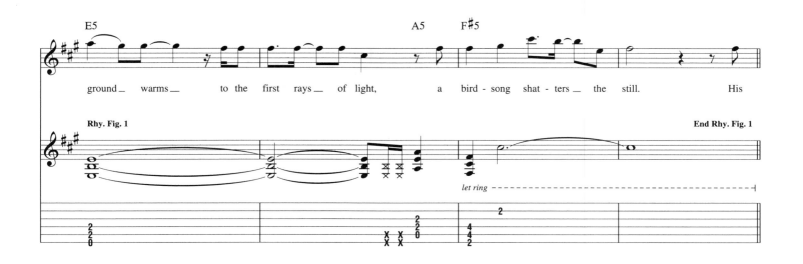

ground__ warms__ to the first rays__ of light, a bird-song shat-ters__ the still. His

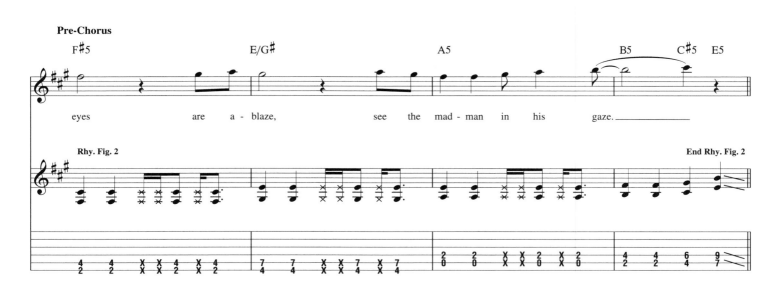

Pre-Chorus

eyes are a-blaze, see the mad-man in his gaze._____

Chorus

Fly on your way like an ea-gle, fly as high as the

Gtrs. 1 & 2: w/ Rhy. Fig. 3

sun. On your way like an ea-gle, fly, touch the

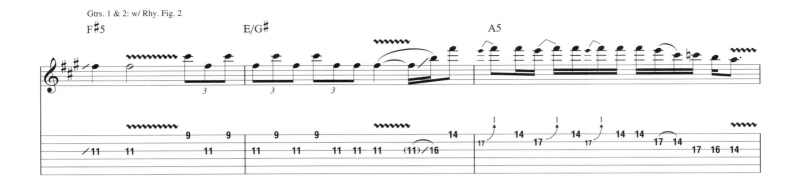

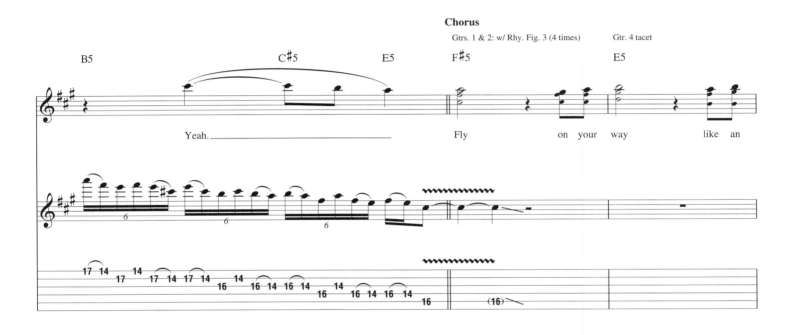

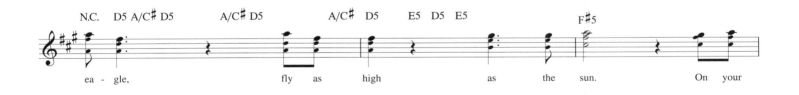

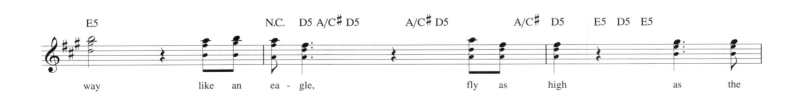

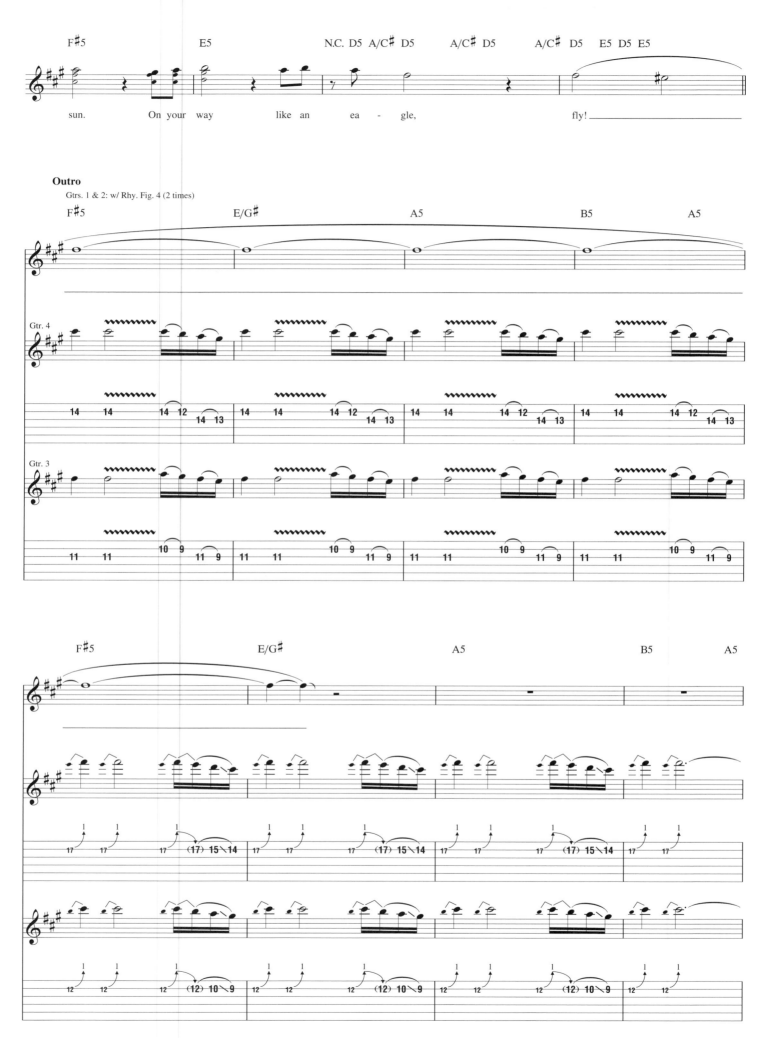

Outro

Gtrs. 1 & 2: w/ Rhy. Fig. 4 (2 times)

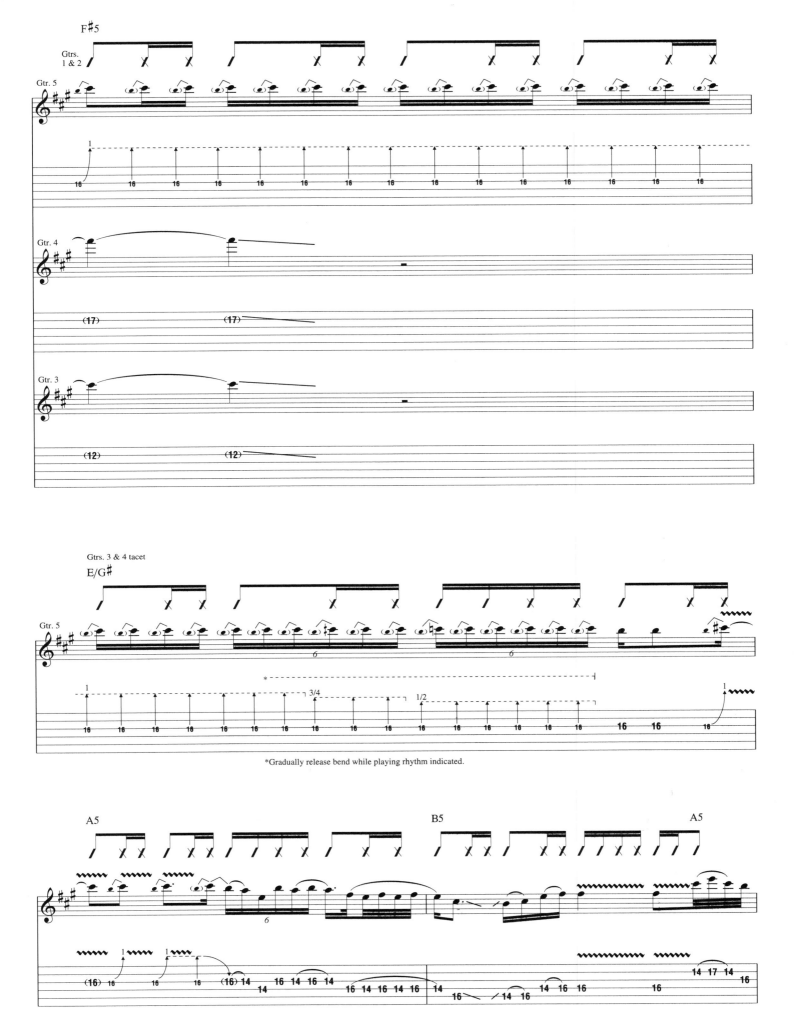

*Gradually release bend while playing rhythm indicated.

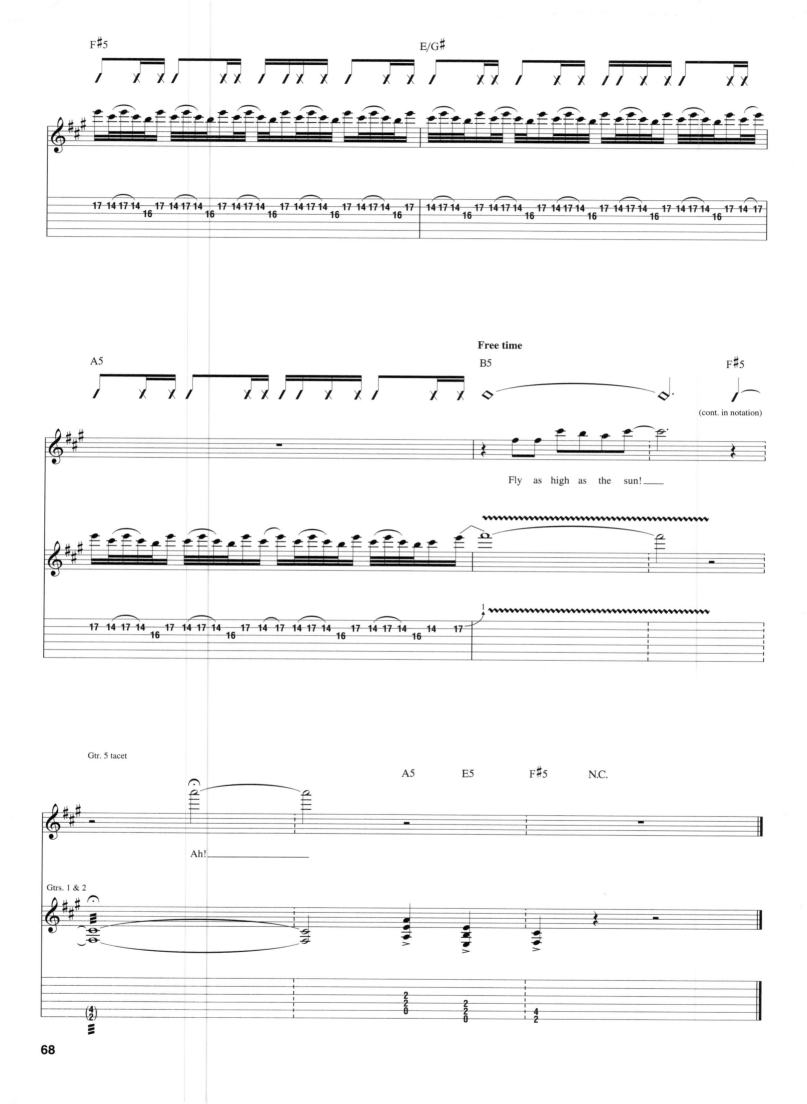

from *Killers*

Killers

Words and Music by Steven Harris and Paul Andrews

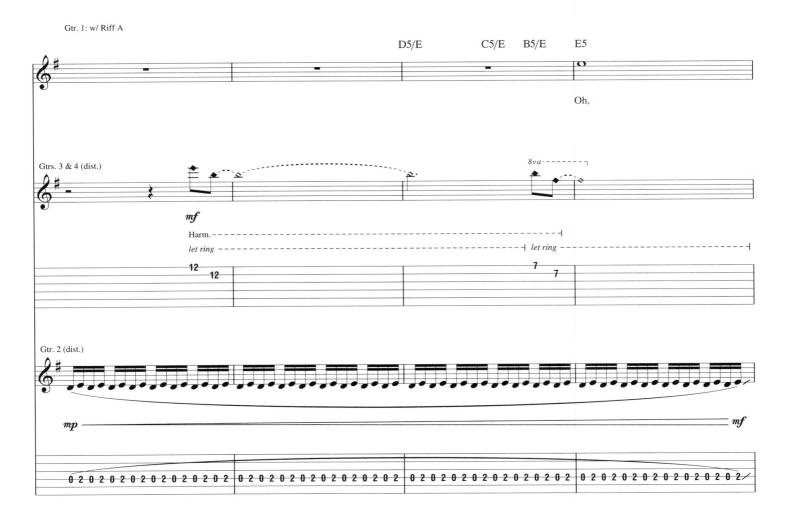

*Bass arr. for gtr. **Chord symbols reflect implied harmony.

Copyright © 1981 by Iron Maiden Holdings Ltd.
All Rights in the world Administered by Zomba Music Publishers Ltd.
All Rights in the United States and Canada Administered by Zomba Enterprises, Inc.
International Copyright Secured   All Rights Reserved

Gtr. 1: w/ Riff A (2 times)
2nd time, Gtrs. 2 & 4: w/ Rhy. Fills 1 & 1A
2nd time, Gtr. 3: w/ Fill 1
E5
D5/E
C5/E
B5/E
E5
yeah,
yeah!
Gtr. 5 (clean)
mf
let ring throughout
Riff B
End Riff B
Gtr. 3
loco
Rhy. Fig. 1
End Rhy. Fig. 1
Gtrs. 2 & 4
loco
f
Rhy. Fill 1
Gtr. 2
Gtr. 4
divisi
Rhy. Fill 1A
Fill 1
Gtr. 3

Gtr. 2: w/ Rhy. Fig. 1
Gtr. 3: w/ Riff B

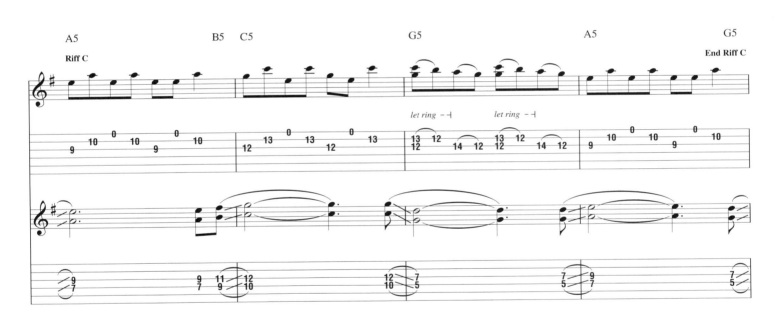

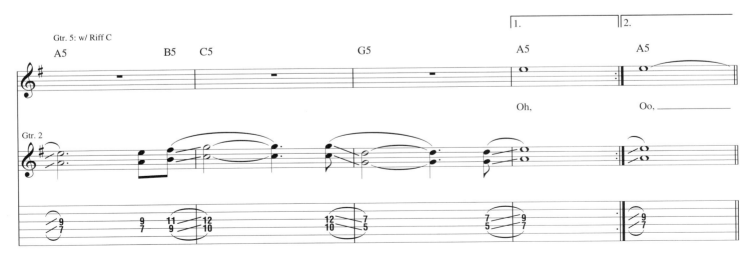

71

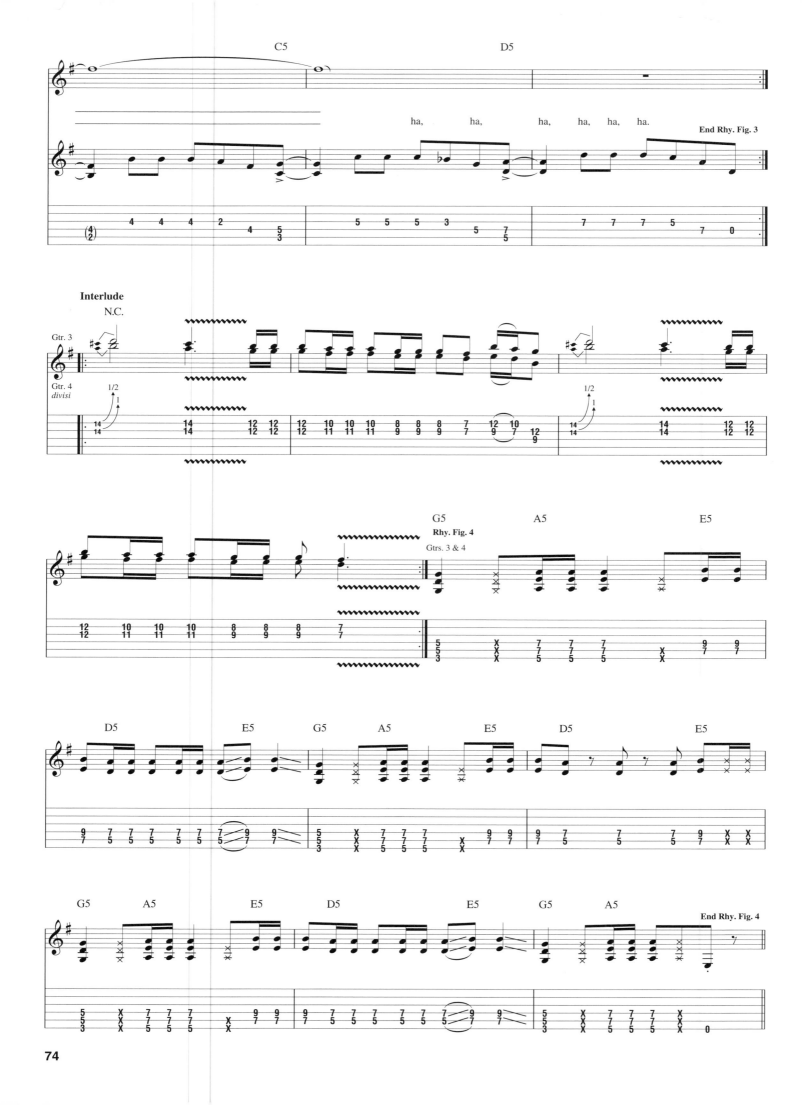

to fore - see, see, ___ see.

Guitar Solo

Ha, ___ ha, ha, ha. ___

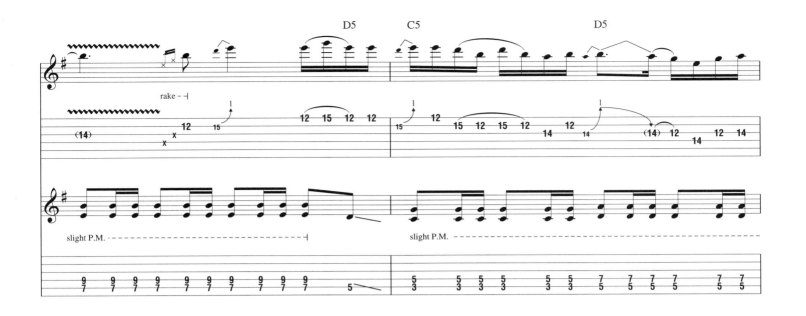

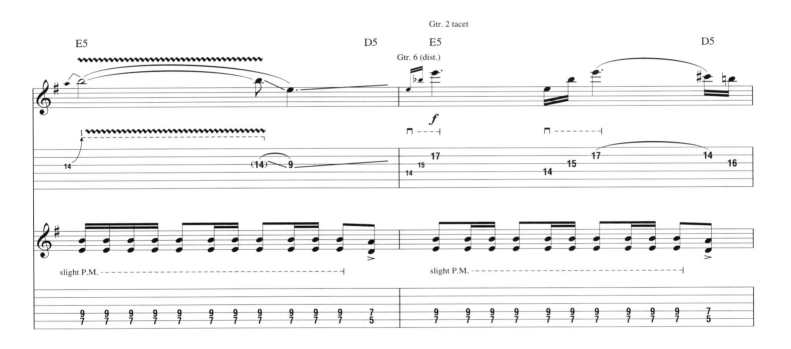

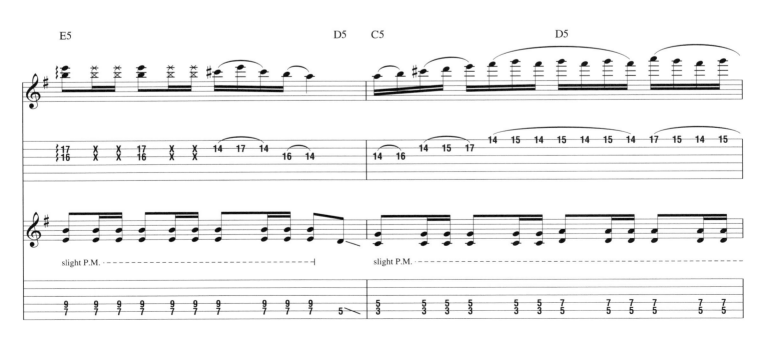

78

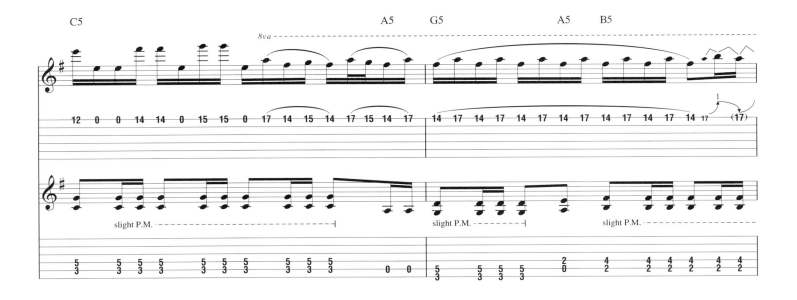

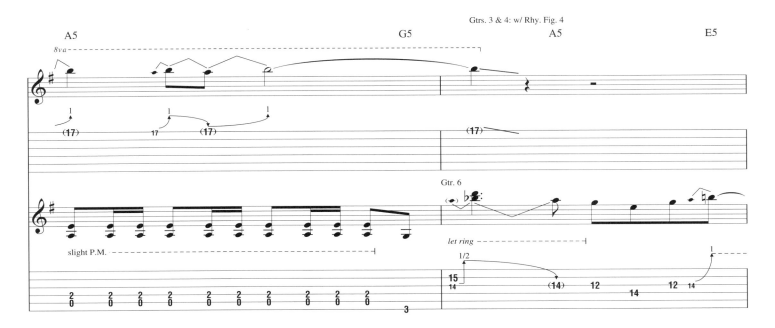

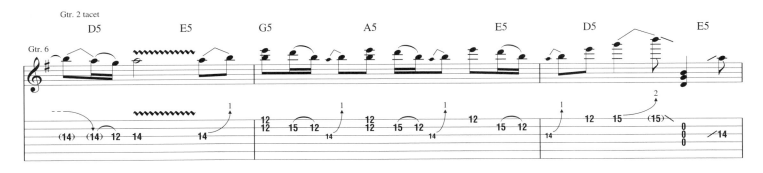

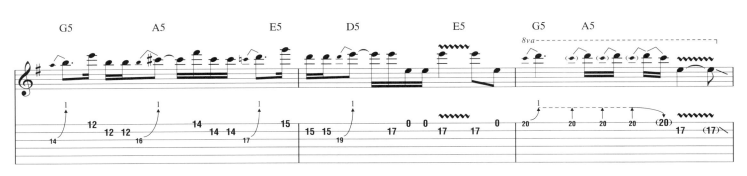

Gtrs. 2 & 6 tacet

ties.

The glim - mer ___ of met - al, ___ my

Gtr. 6

(7)

Gtr. 2

(7)

mo - ment ___ is read - y ___ to strike. ___ The

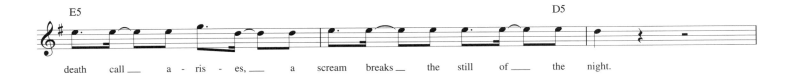

death call ___ a - ris - es, ___ a scream breaks ___ the still of ___ the night.

An - oth - er ___ to - mor - row, ___ re - mem - ber to walk in ___ the

Chorus

Gtrs. 3 & 4: w/ Rhy. Fig. 3

light. ___   I   have found ___

81

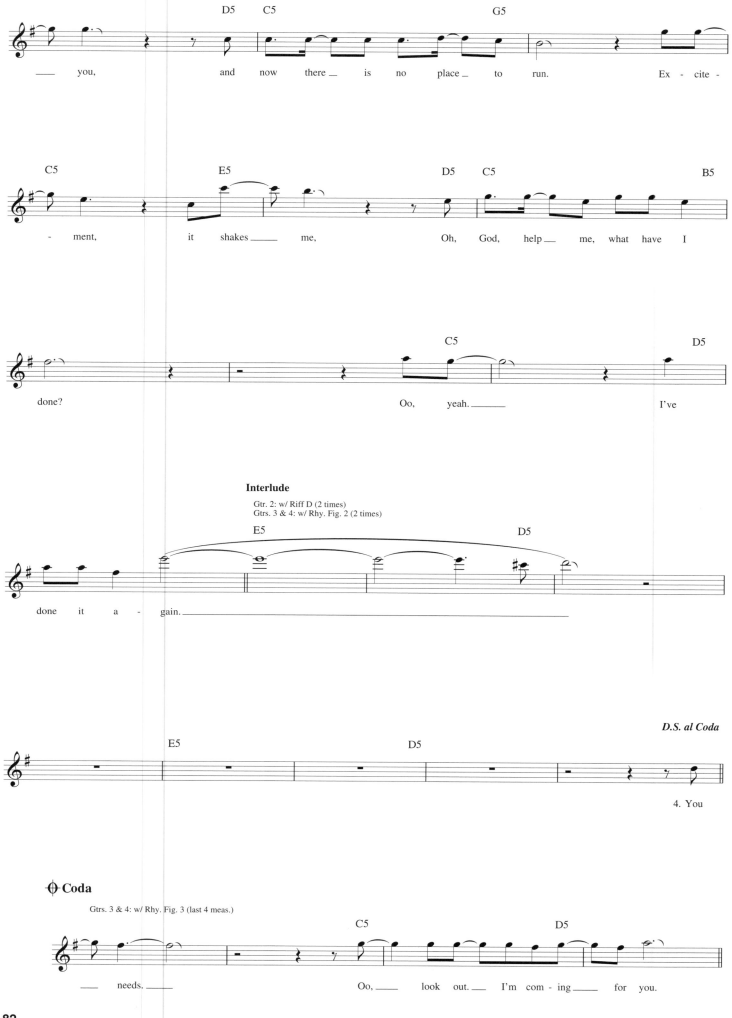

you, and now there ___ is no place ___ to run. Ex - cite -

- ment, it shakes ___ me, Oh, God, help ___ me, what have I

done? Oo, yeah. ___ I've

Interlude

Gtr. 2: w/ Riff D (2 times)
Gtrs. 3 & 4: w/ Rhy. Fig. 2 (2 times)

done it a - gain. ___

D.S. al Coda

4. You

⊕ **Coda**

Gtrs. 3 & 4: w/ Rhy. Fig. 3 (last 4 meas.)

___ needs. ___ Oo, ___ look out. I'm com - ing ___ for you.

Outro

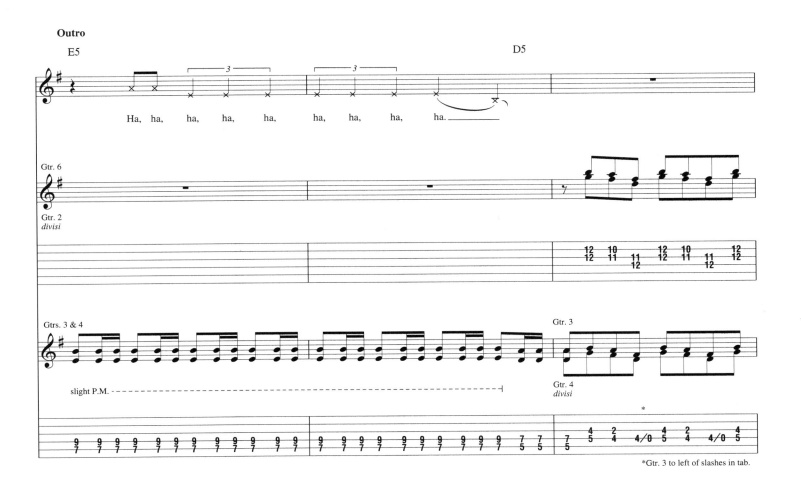

Ha, ha, ha, ha, ha, ha, ha, ha, ha.

*Gtr. 3 to left of slashes in tab.

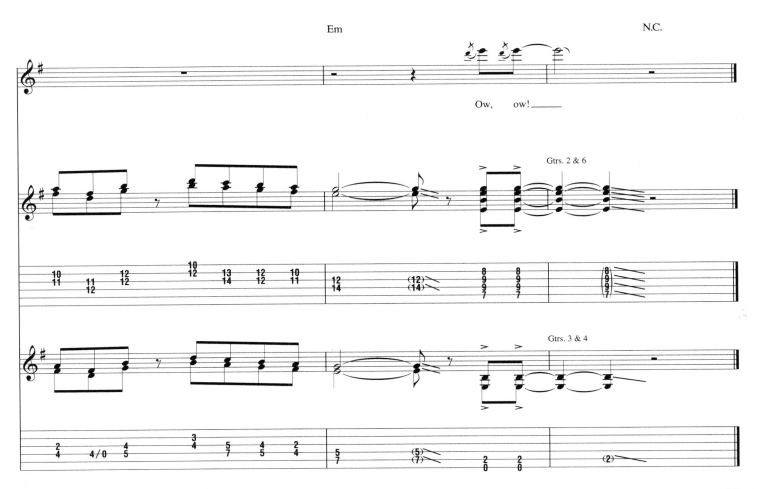

Ow, ow!

from *No Prayer for the Dying*

No Prayer For the Dying

Words and Music by Steven Harris

Copyright © 1990 by Iron Maiden Holdings Ltd.
All Rights in the world Administered by Zomba Music Publishers Ltd.
All Rights in the United States and Canada Administered by Zomba Enterprises, Inc.
International Copyright Secured   All Rights Reserved

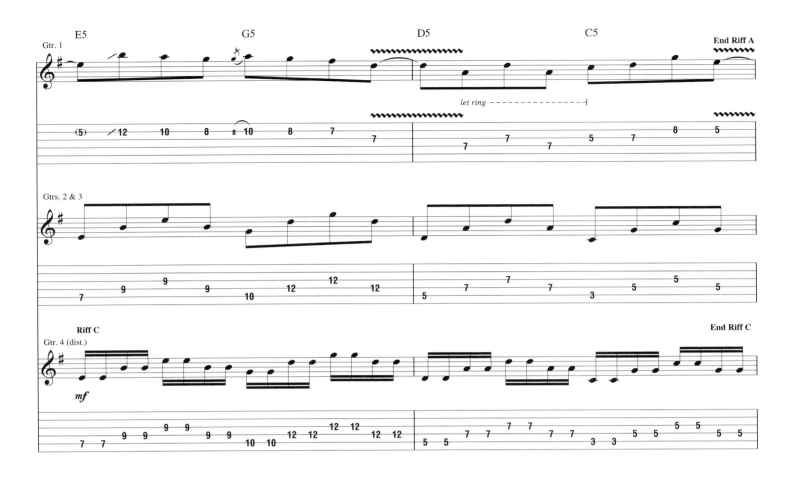

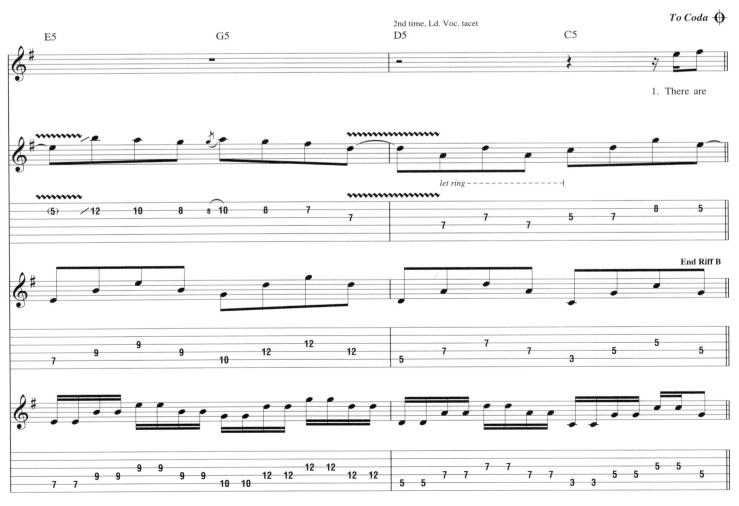

some-thing to bet on, ____ you've got noth-ing ____ to lose, ____ yeah.
walk-ing a long _____ road nev-er reach-ing ____ the end.

Gtr. 6 (dist.)

mf

Gtr. 2

Interlude

Gtr. 2 tacet

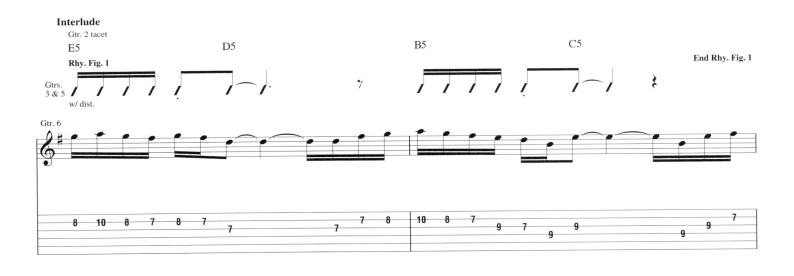

Rhy. Fig. 1

Gtrs.
3 & 5
w/ dist.

E5   D5   B5   C5

End Rhy. Fig. 1

Gtr. 6

Gtrs. 3 & 5: w/ Rhy. Fig. 1 (2 times)

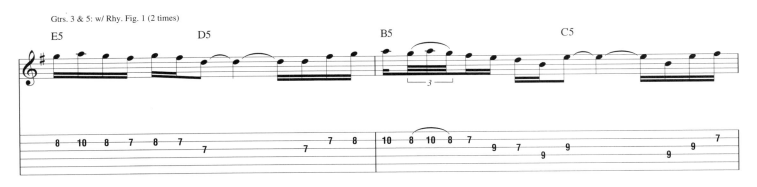

E5   D5   B5   C5

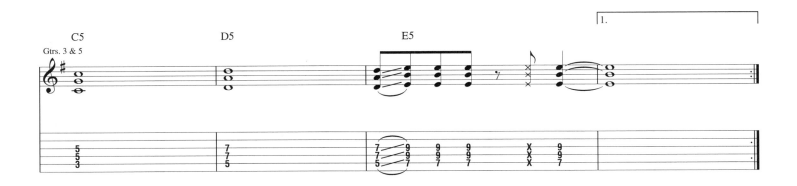

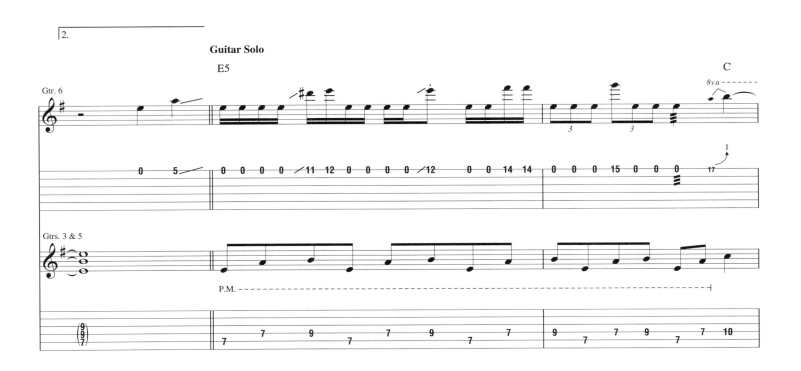

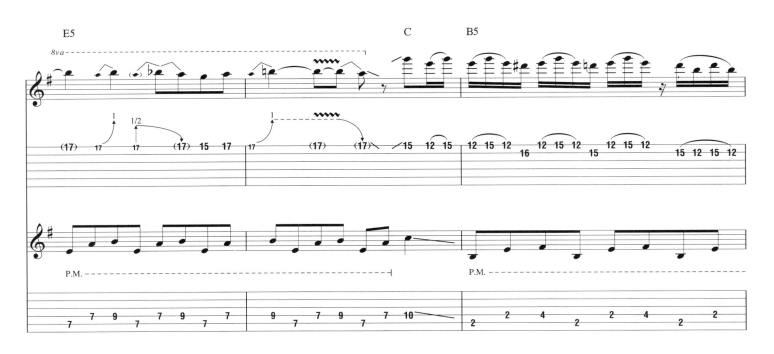

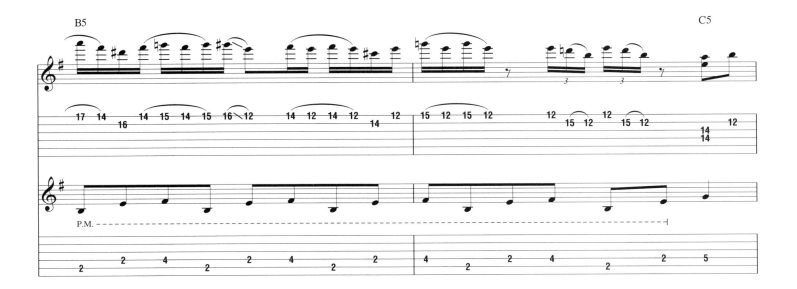

Guitar Solo
Gtrs. 3 & 5: w/ Riff D (1 5/8 times)
Gtr. 6 tacet

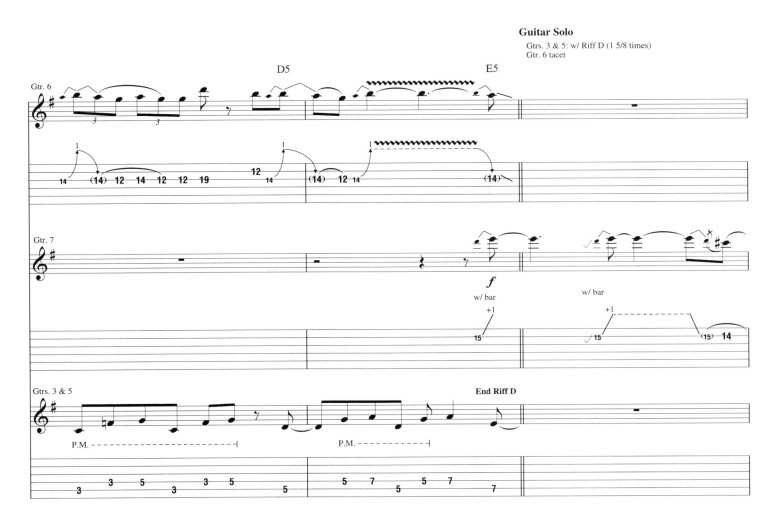

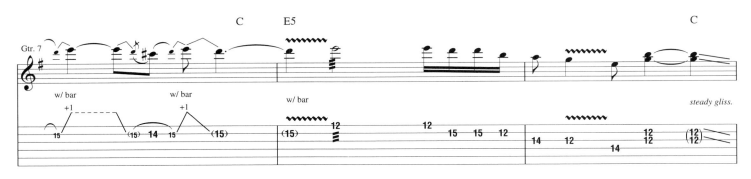

Guitar Solo

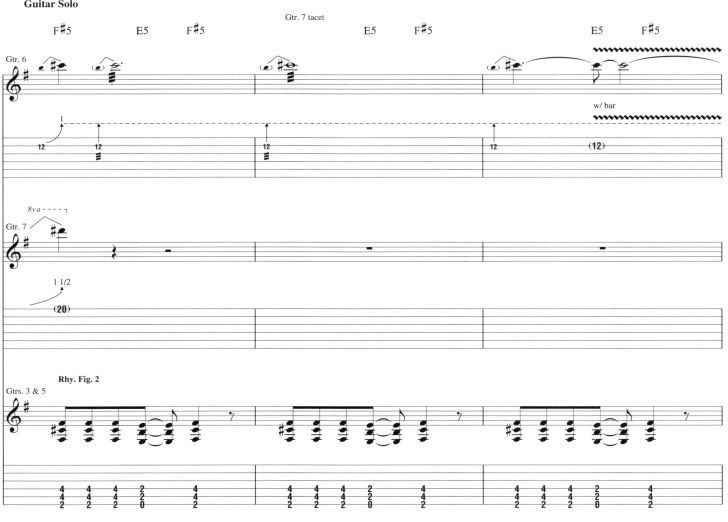

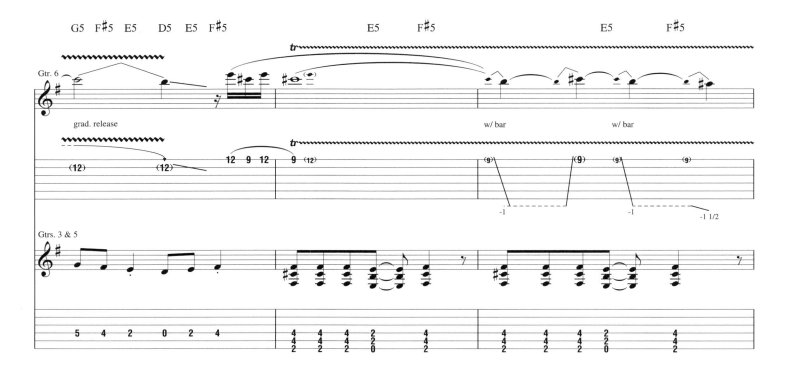

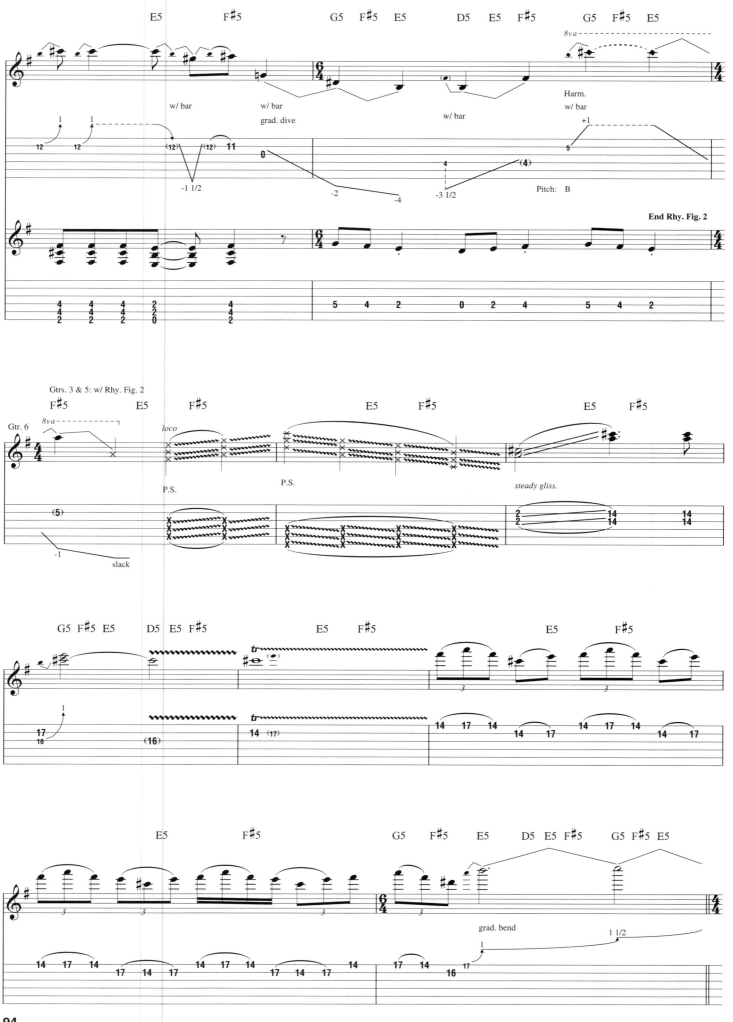

Bridge

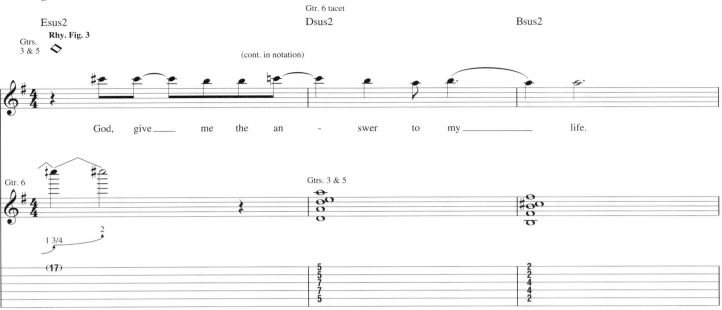

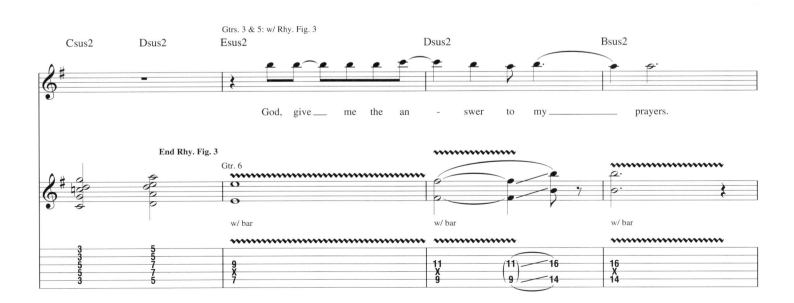

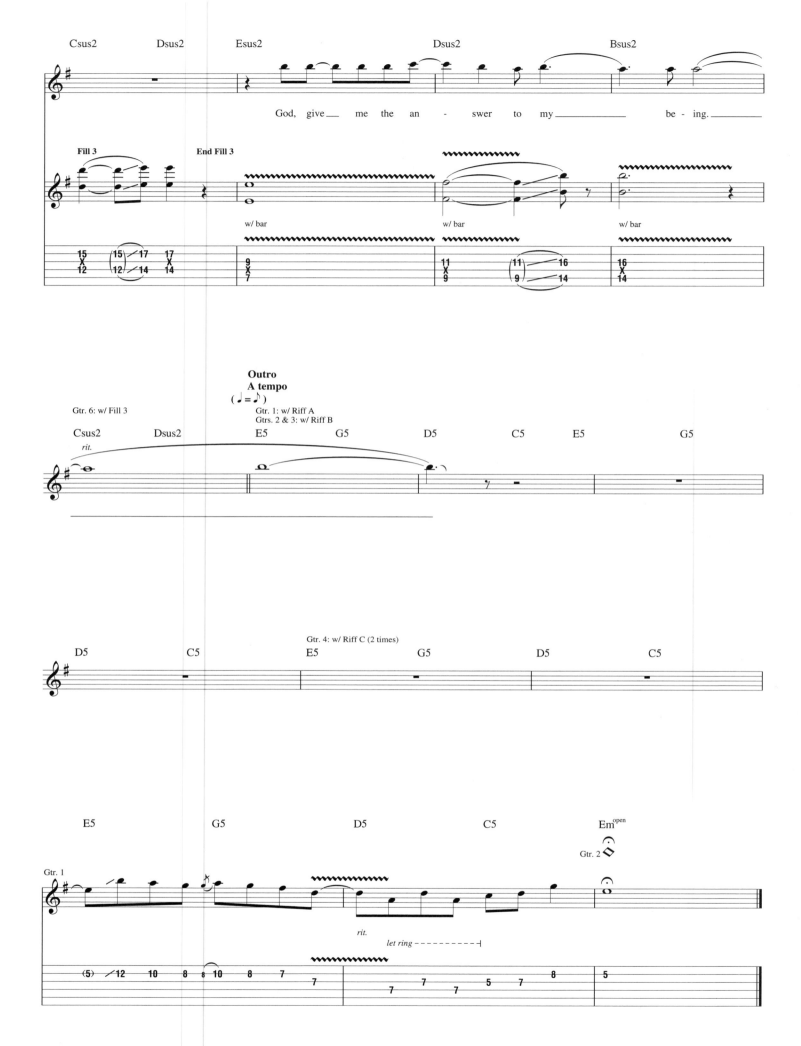

God, give me the an - swer to my be - ing.

The Number of the Beast

Words and Music by Steven Harris

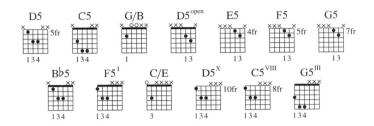

Spoken: Woe to you, oh, Earth and Sea,
For the Devil sends the beast with wrath,
Because he knows the time is short...
Let him who hath understanding
Reckon the number of the beast,
For it is a human number.
Its number is six hundred and sixty six.

- Revelations Ch. 13 v. 8

Intro
Fast Rock ♩ = 195

*Chord symbols reflect overall harmony.

Copyright © 1982 by Iron Maiden Holdings Ltd.
All Rights in the world Administered by Zomba Music Publishers Ltd.
All Rights in the United States and Canada Administered by Zomba Enterprises, Inc.
International Copyright Secured All Rights Reserved

Verse

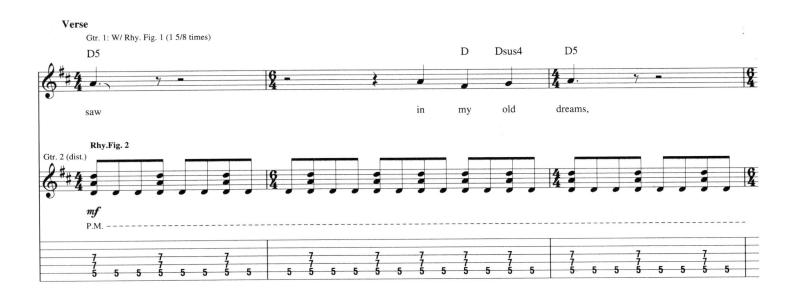

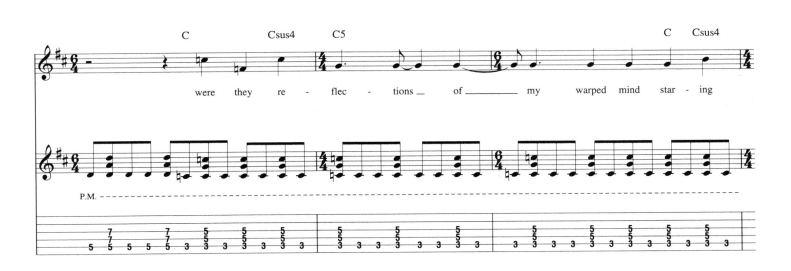

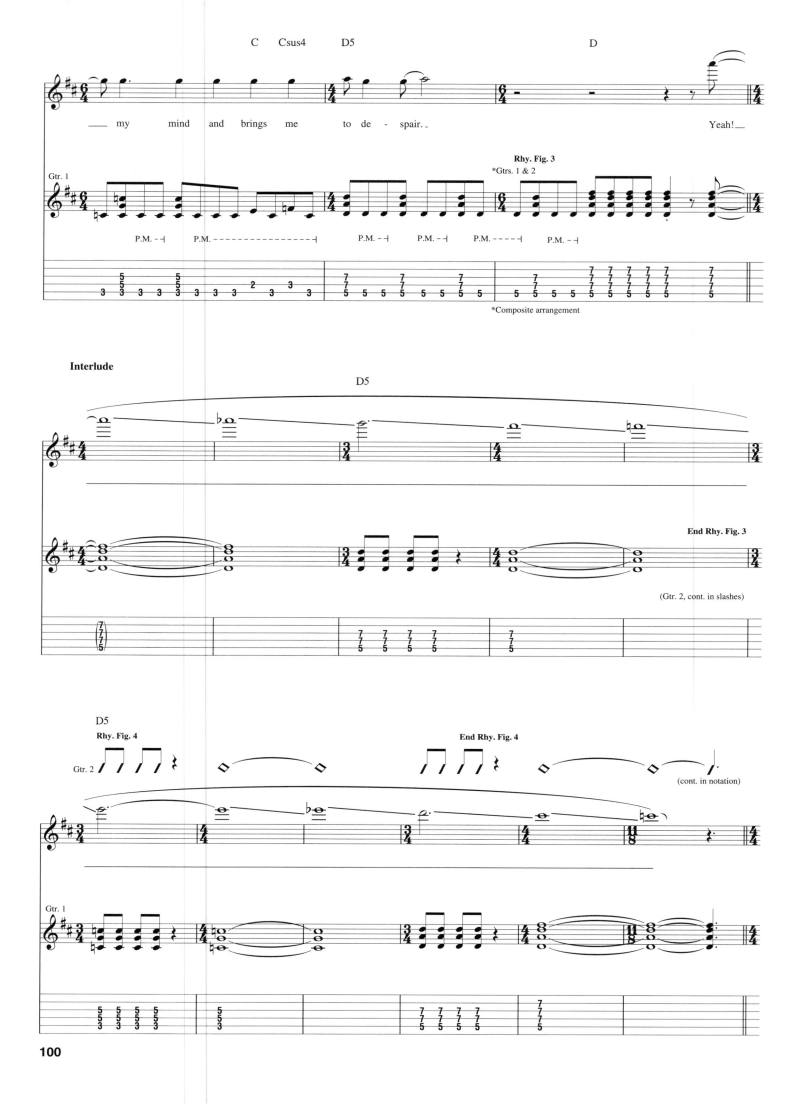

my mind and brings me to de - spair.

Yeah!

Interlude

Chorus

Interlude

*Voc. tacet on repeats.

Guitar Solo

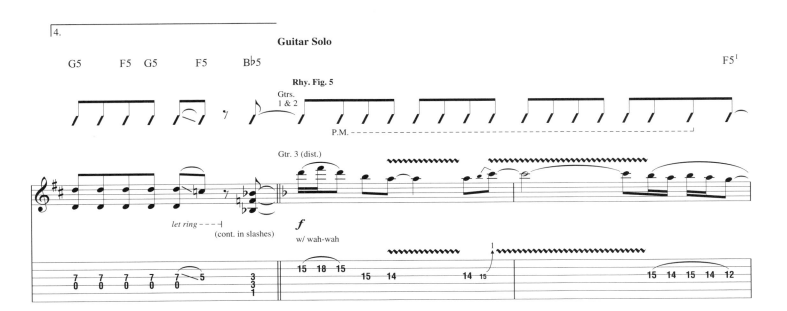

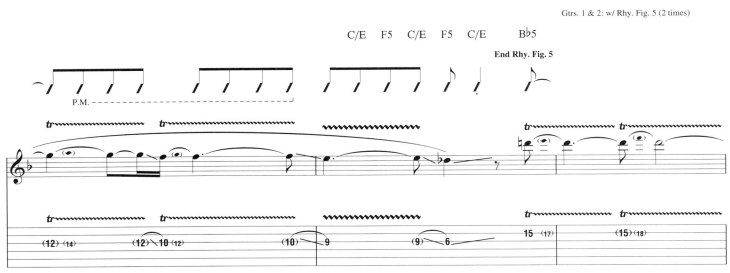

Interlude

104

Guitar Solo

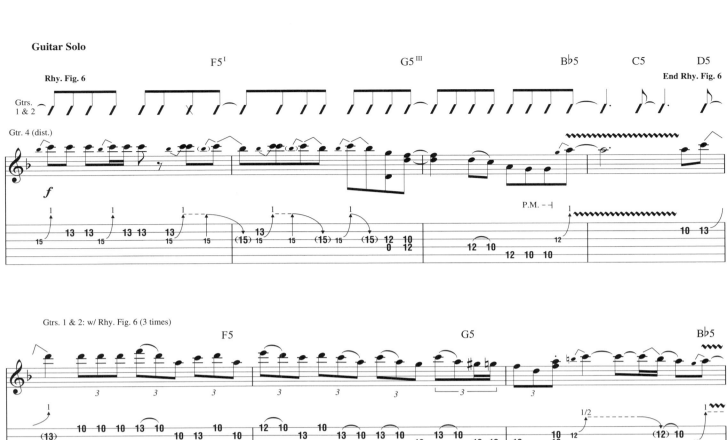

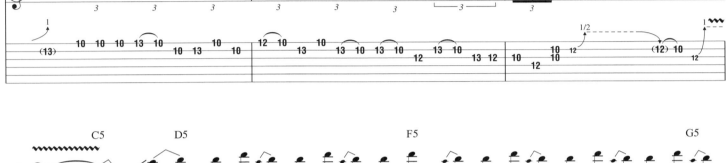

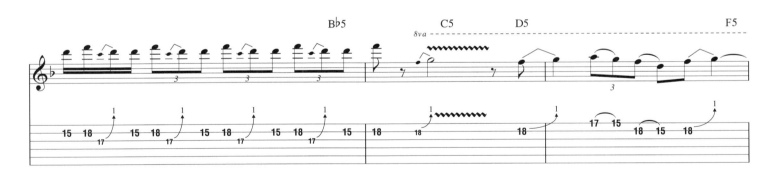

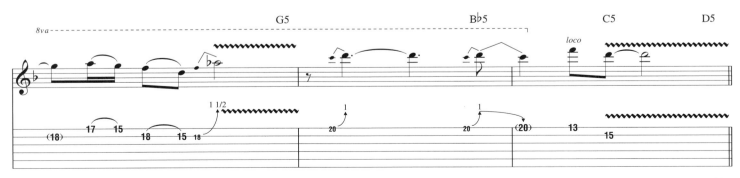

Interlude

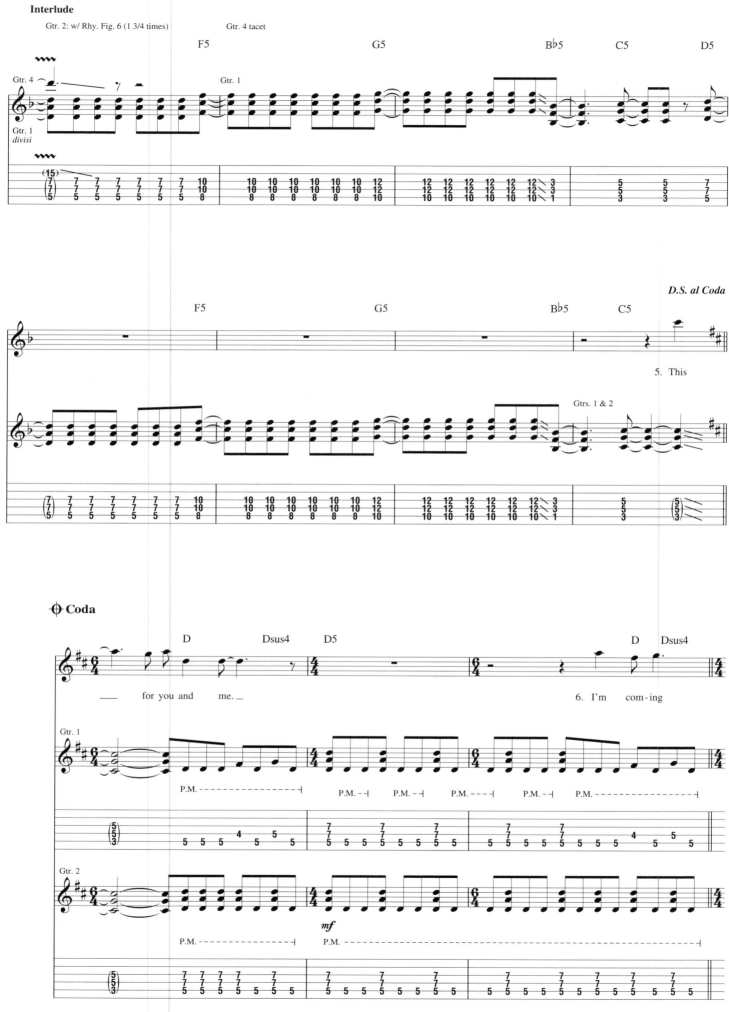

Verse

Gtr. 1 : w/ Rhy. Fig. 1 (1 7/8 times)
Gtr. 2: w/ Rhy. Fig. 2 (1 7/8 times)

back.   I will re - turn._____   And I'll pos -

sess your__ bod - y   and I'll make you burn.   I have the

fire.   I have the force.   I have the

pow - er to _____ make   my e - vil take its course.

Outro

Gtr. 2: w/ Rhy. Fig. 3

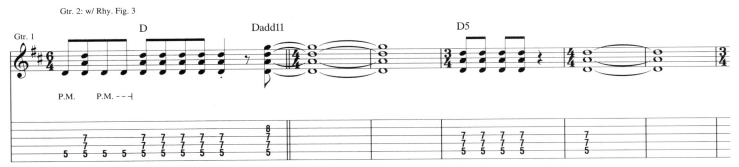

Gtr. 2: w/ Rhy. Fig. 4

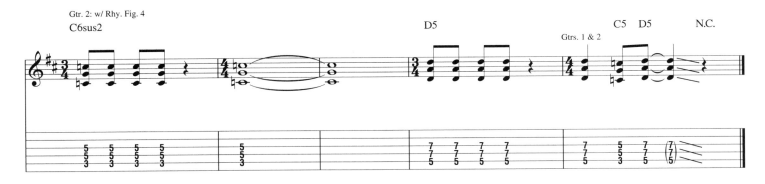

from *Iron Maiden*

The Phantom of the Opera

Words and Music by Steven Harris

Copyright © 1980 by Iron Maiden Holdings Ltd.
All Rights in the world Administered by Zomba Music Publishers Ltd.
All Rights in the United States and Canada Administered by Zomba Enterprises, Inc.
International Copyright Secured   All Rights Reserved

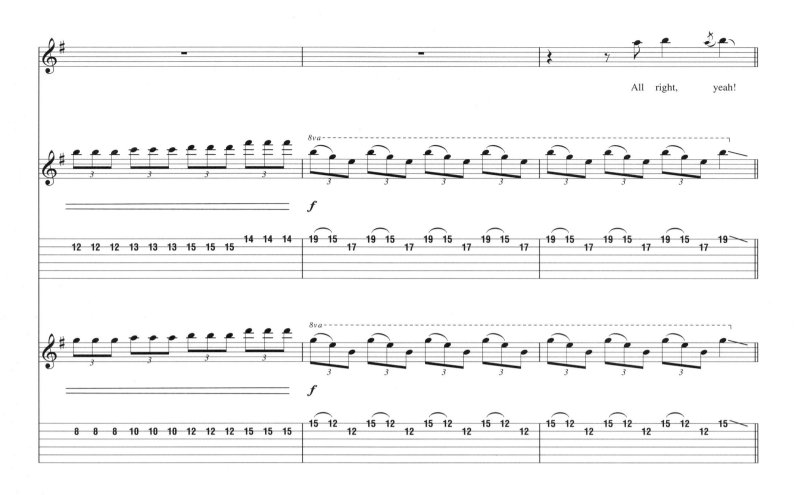

All right, yeah!

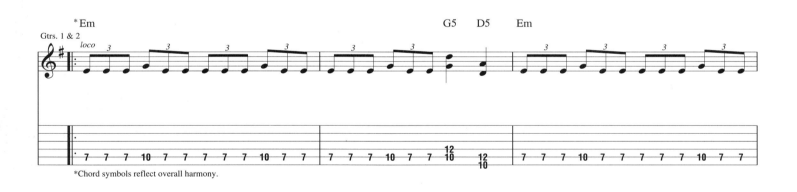

*Em   G5   D5   Em

Gtrs. 1 & 2

*Chord symbols reflect overall harmony.

G5   D5   F#m   Gm

Play 3 times

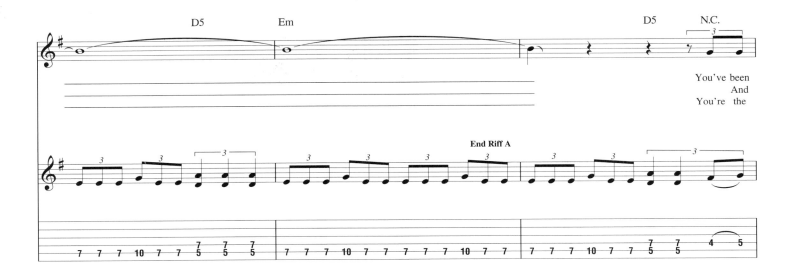

You've been
And
You're the

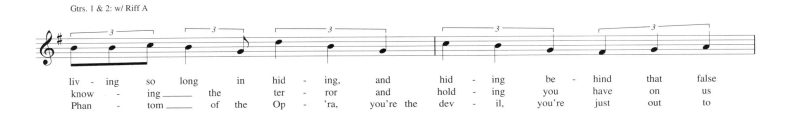

Gtrs. 1 & 2: w/ Riff A

liv - ing so long in hid - ing, and hid - ing be - hind that false
know - ing the ter - ror and hold - ing you have on us
Phan - tom of the Op - 'ra, you're the dev - il, you're just out to

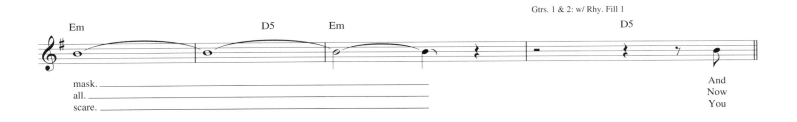

Gtrs. 1 & 2: w/ Rhy. Fill 1

mask. And
all. Now
scare. You

Chorus

Gtrs. 1 & 2: w/ Rhy. Fig. 1

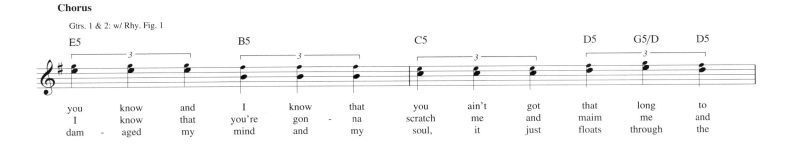

you know and I know that you ain't got that long to
I know and that you're gon - na you scratch me and just maim me to and
dam - aged my mind and my soul, it just floats through the

To Coda ⊕

Gtrs. 1 & 2: w/ Rhy. Fill 1

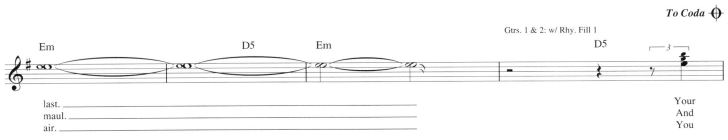

last. Your
maul. And
air. You

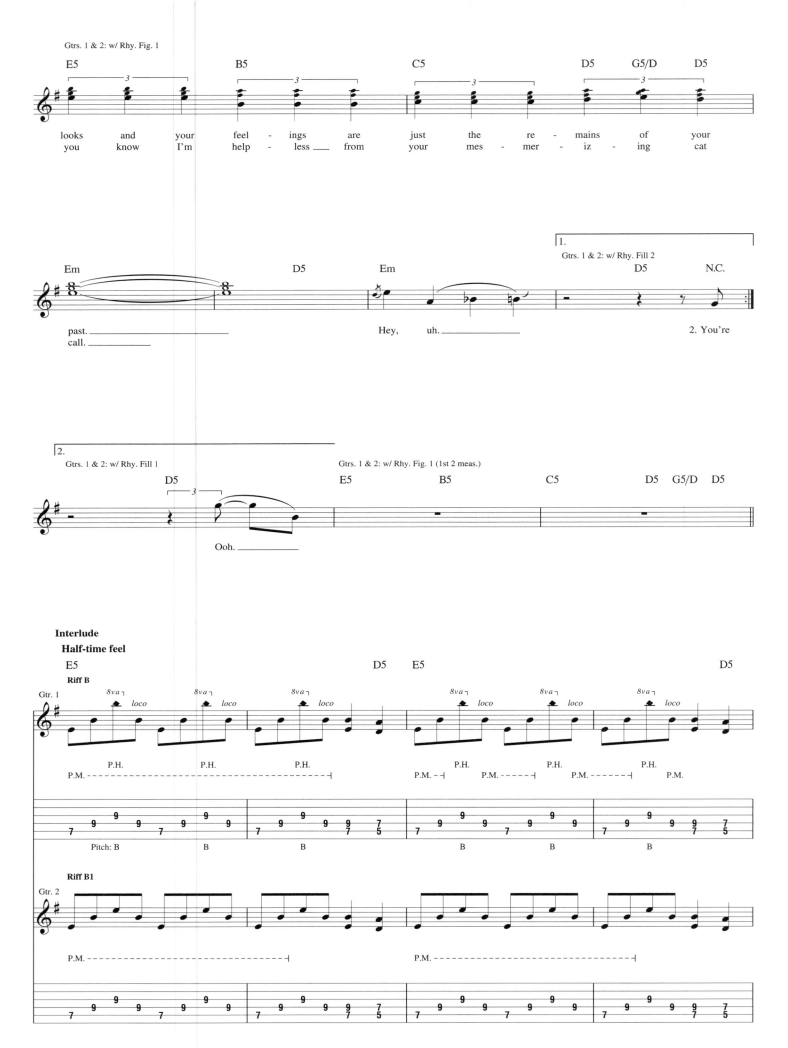

*T = Thumb on 6th string

*Flip pickup selector
switch from neck to
bridge position.

117

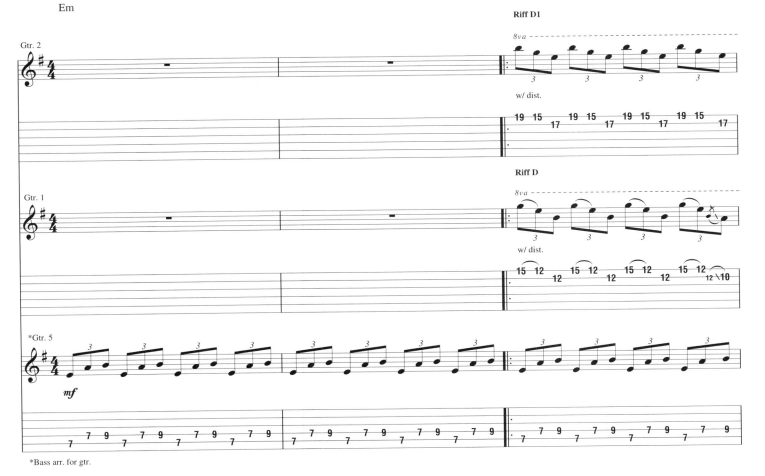

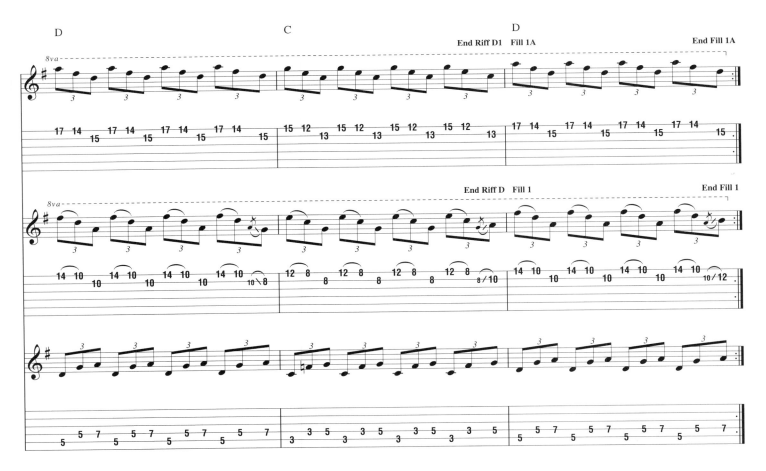

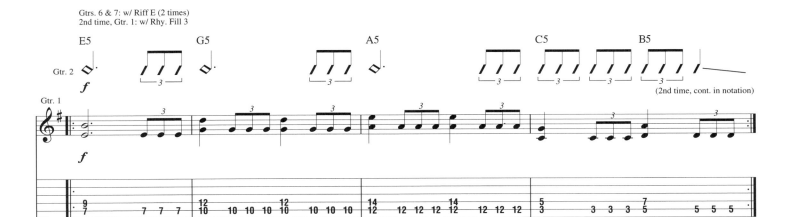

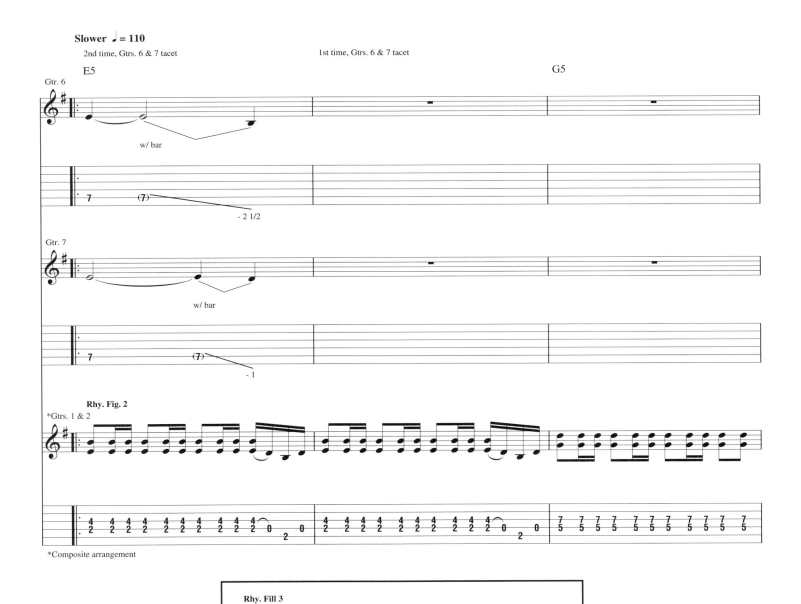

*Composite arrangement

122

Guitar Solo

Gtrs. 6 & 7 tacet

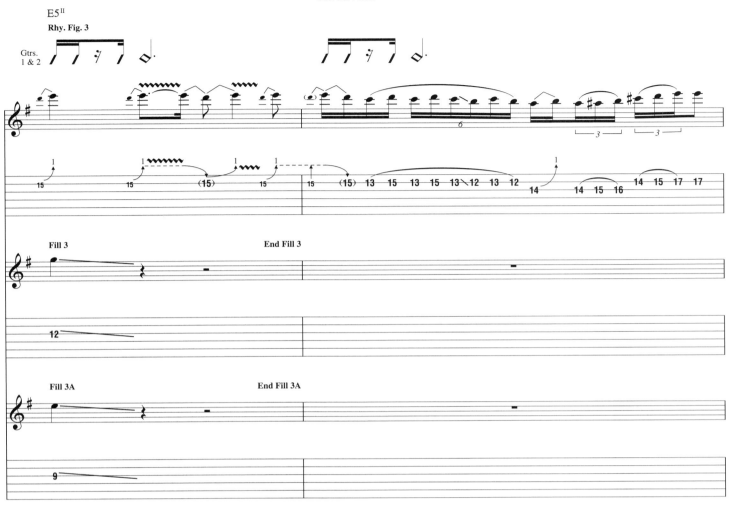

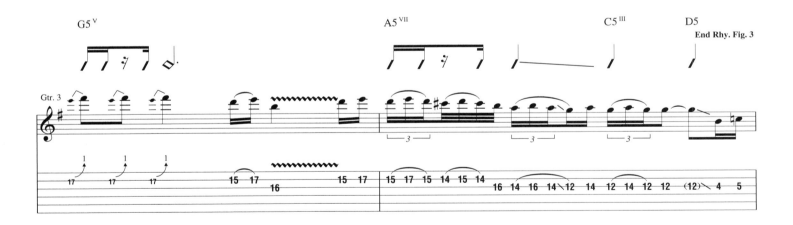

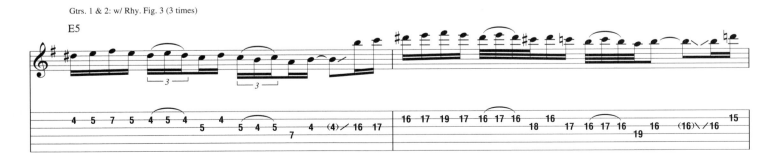

Interlude

Gtrs. 1 & 2: w/ Rhy. Fig. 2 (2 times)
Gtrs. 6 & 7: w/ Riffs F & F1

Gtr. 4 tacet

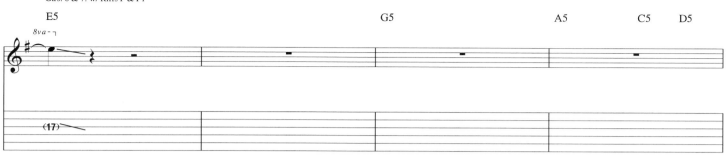

*2nd time, D.S. al Coda
(take repeats)

Gtrs. 1 & 2: w/ Rhy. Fig. 2 (2 times)
1st time, Gtrs. 6 & 7: w/ Fills 3 & 3A

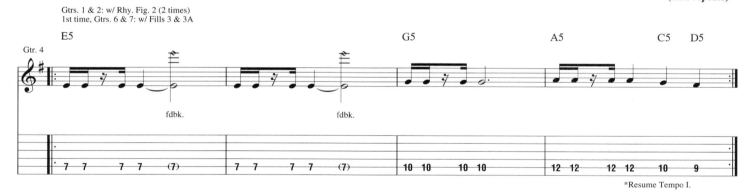

*Resume Tempo I.

Coda

haunt me, you taunt me, you tor - ture me back at your lair!

Gtrs. 1 & 2

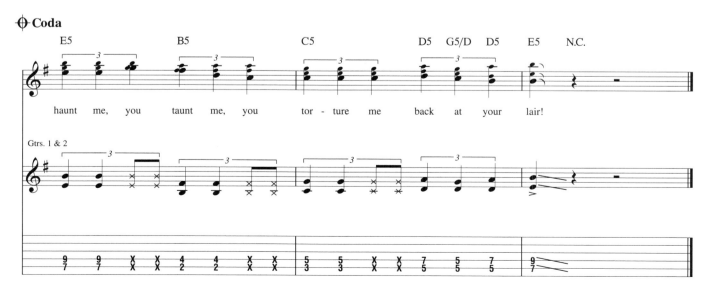

from *Piece of Mind*

Revelations

Words and Music by Bruce Dickinson

Copyright © 1983 by Iron Maiden Holdings Ltd.
All Rights in the world Administered by Zomba Music Publishers Ltd.
All Rights in the United States and Canada Administered by Zomba Enterprises, Inc.
International Copyright Secured   All Rights Reserved

down and hear our cry. Our earth-ly rul-ers fal-ter, our peo-ple drift and die. __ The

walls of gold en-tomb __ us, the swords __ of scorn di-vide. __ Take not thy thun-der from __ us, but

Interlude

Gtrs. 1 & 2 tacet

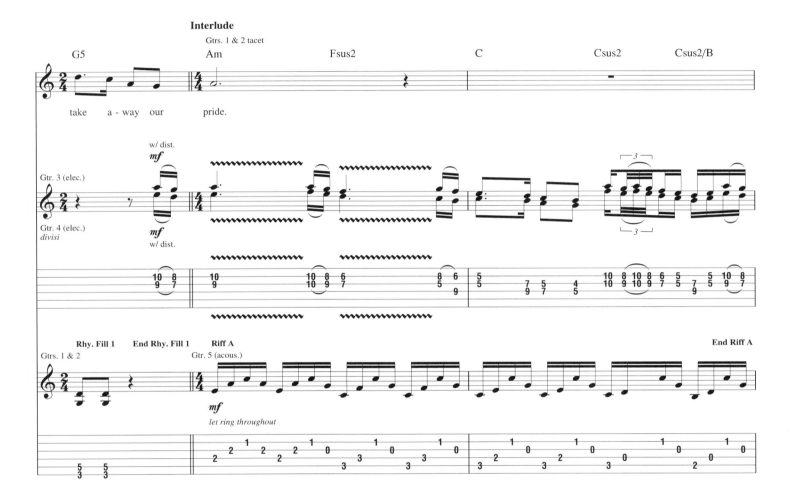

take a-way our pride.

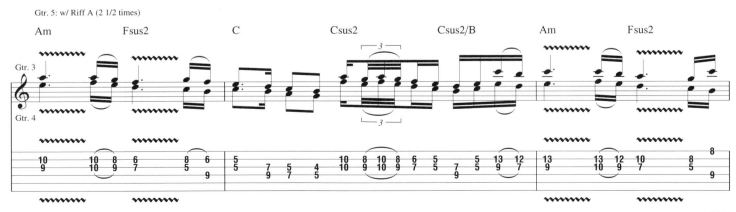

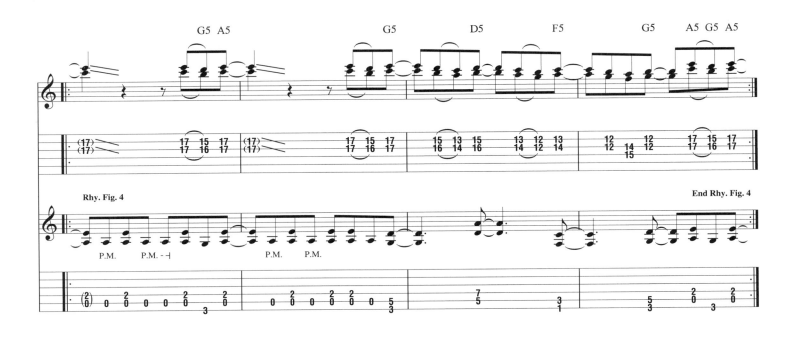

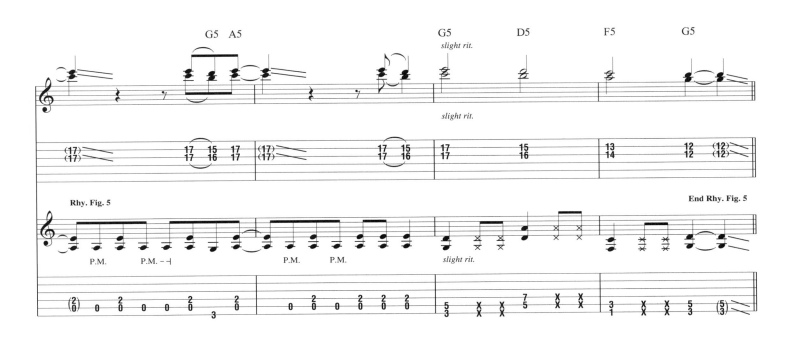

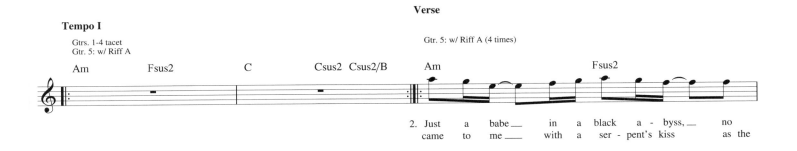

Verse

Tempo I

Gtrs. 1-4 tacet
Gtr. 5: w/ Riff A

Gtr. 5: w/ Riff A (4 times)

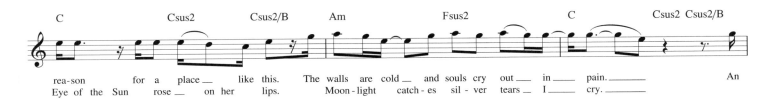

2. Just a babe in a black a - byss, no
came to me with a ser - pent's kiss as the

rea - son for a place like this. The walls are cold and souls cry out in pain.
Eye of the Sun rose on her lips. Moon - light catch - es sil - ver tears I cry. An

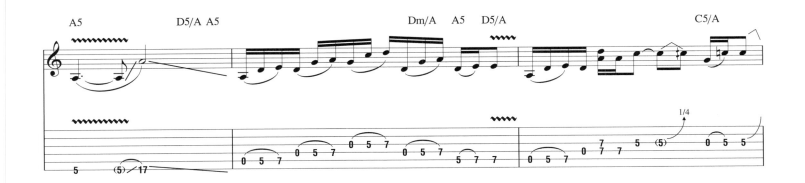

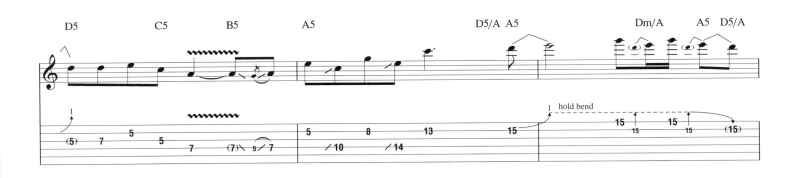

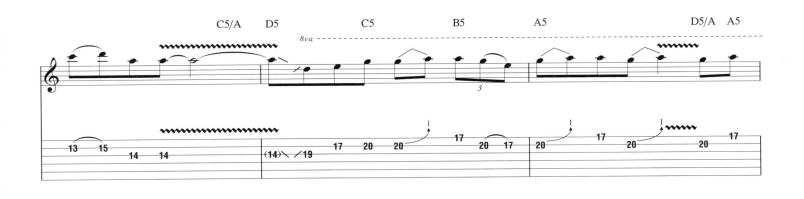

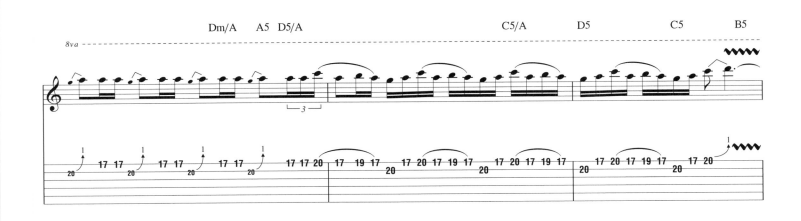

Interlude

Verse

Outro

Run to the Hills

Words and Music by Steven Harris

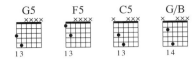

*Composite arrangement

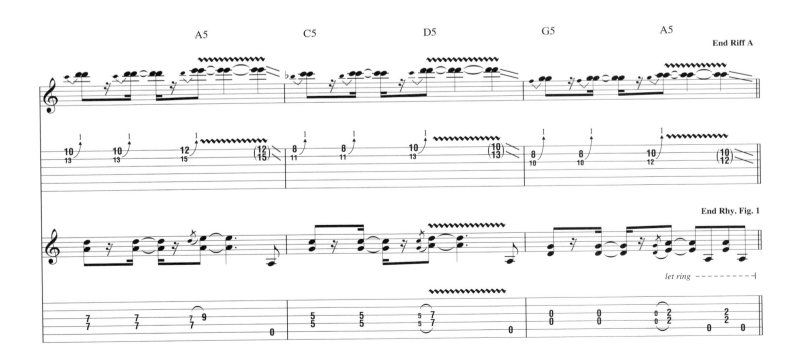

Copyright © 1982 by Iron Maiden Holdings Ltd.
All Rights in the world Administered by Zomba Music Publishers Ltd.
All Rights in the United States Administered by Zomba Enterprises, Inc.
International Copyright Secured   All Rights Reserved

Verse
1st time, Gtr. 3 tacet

2. Rid - ing through dust _ clouds and bar - ren wastes, _
3. Sol - dier blue _____ in the bar - ren wastes, _

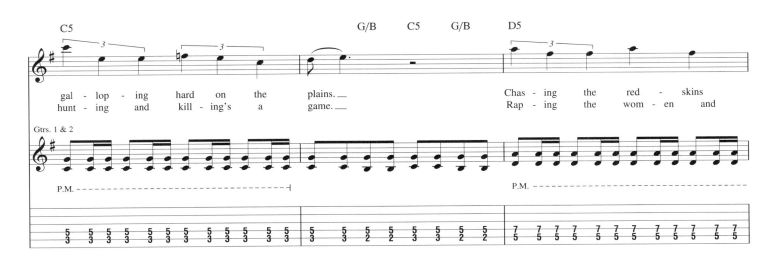

gal - lop - ing hard on the plains. _ Chas - ing the red - skins
hunt - ing and kill - ing's a game. _ Rap - ing the wom - en and

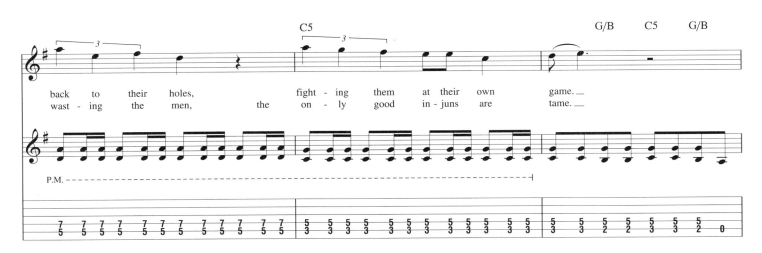

back to their holes, fight - ing them at their own game. _
wast - ing the men, the on - ly good in - juns are tame. _

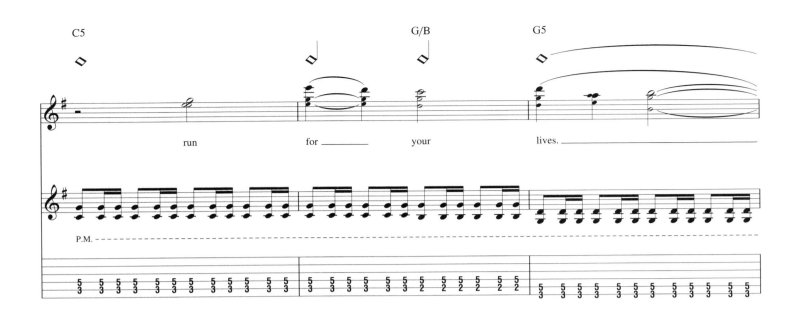

run   for _____ your   lives. _____

Gtrs. 1 & 2: w/ Rhy. Figs. 2 & 2A (1st 6 meas.)

Run   to   the   hills,

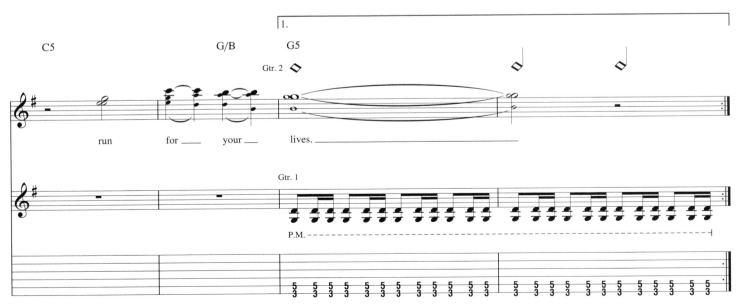

run   for ___ your ___   lives. _____

Gtrs. 1 & 2: w/ Rhy. Fig. 3 (3 times)

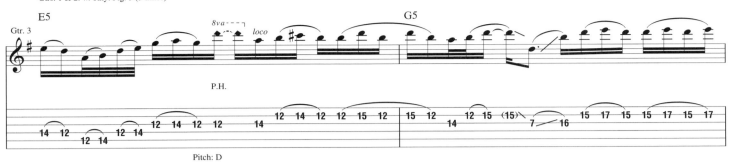

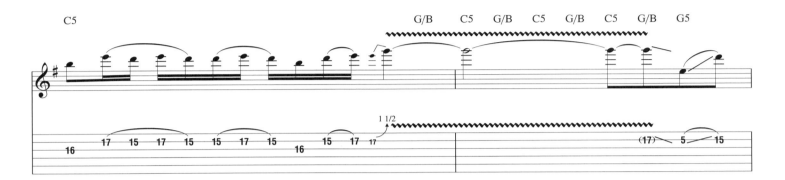

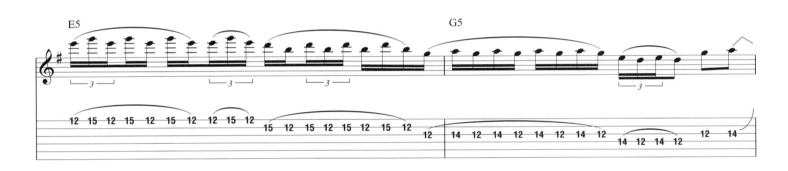

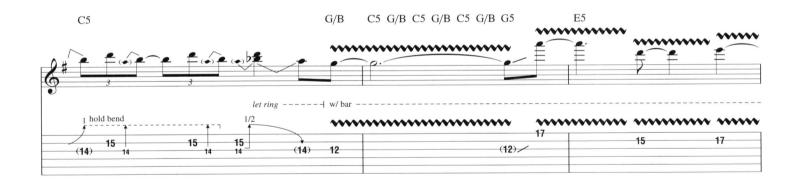

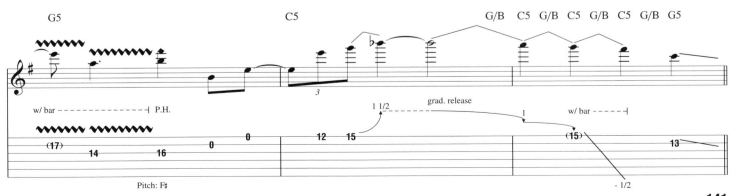

142

F5

Run   to   the   hills,

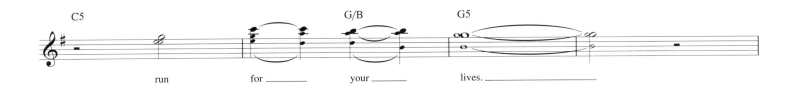

C5   G/B   G5

run   for   your   lives.

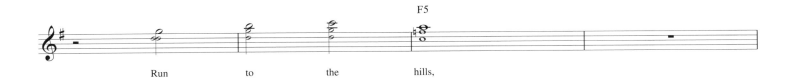

F5

Run   to   the   hills,

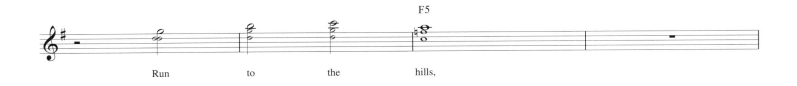

C5   G/B   G5

run   for   your   lives.

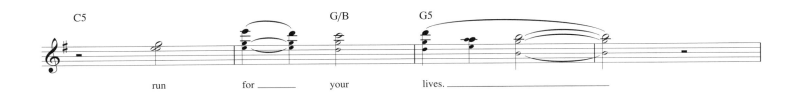

F5

Run   to   the   hills,

Free time

C5   G/B   G5

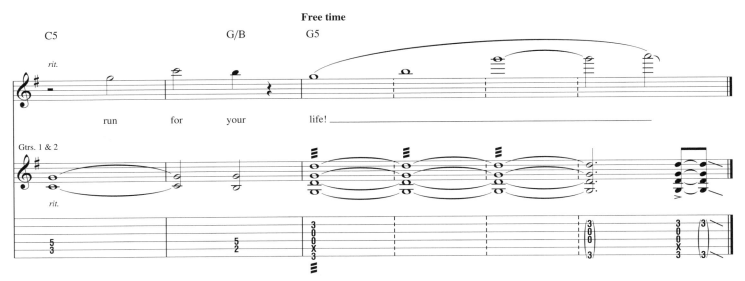

run   for   your   life!

from *Iron Maiden*

Running Free

Words and Music by Steven Harris and Paul Andrews

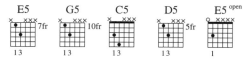

Copyright © 1980 by Iron Maiden Holdings Ltd.
All Rights in the world Administered by Zomba Music Publishers Ltd.
All Rights in the United States and Canada Administered by Zomba Enterprises, Inc.
International Copyright Secured   All Rights Reserved

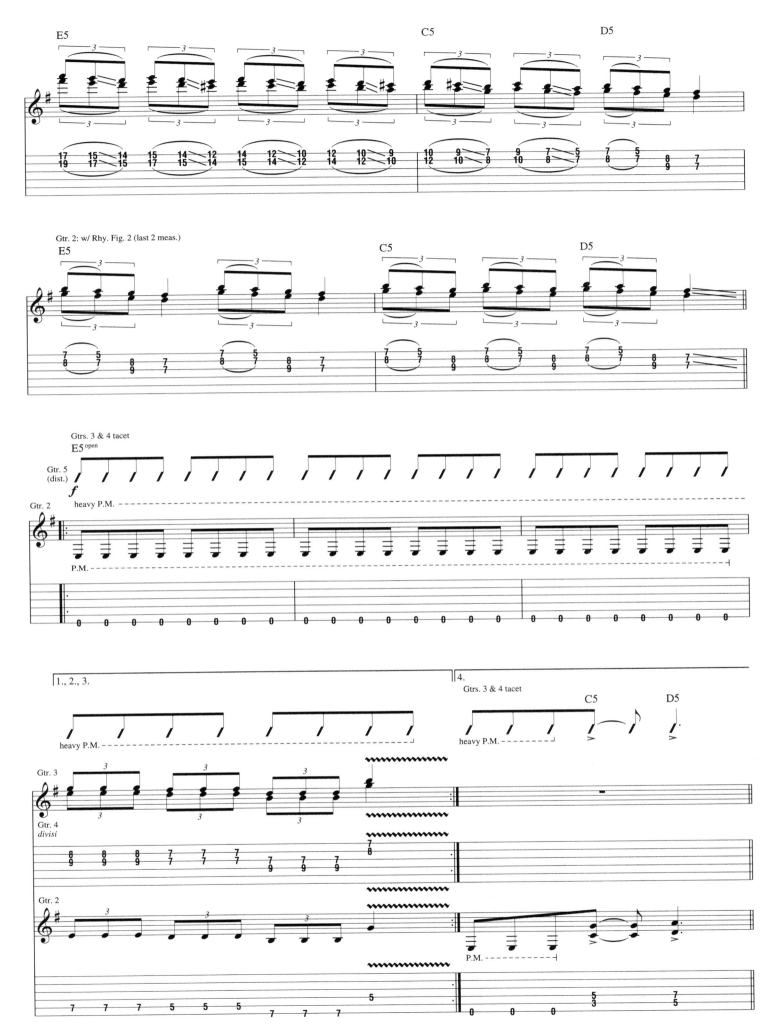

from *Piece of Mind*

The Trooper

Words and Music by Steven Harris

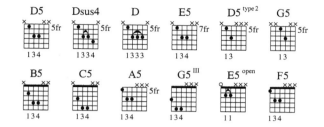

Intro
Moderately fast Rock ♩ = 160

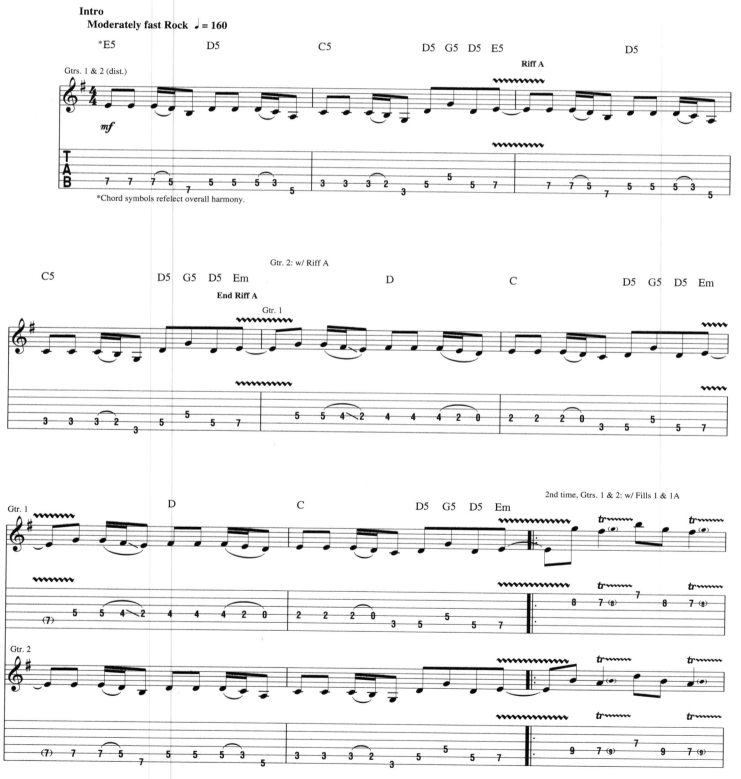

*Chord symbols refelect overall harmony.

Copyright © 1996 by Iron Maiden Holdings Ltd.
All Rights in the world Administered by Zomba Music Publishers Ltd.
All Rights in the United States and Canada Administered by Zomba Enterprises, Inc.
International Copyright Secured   All Rights Reserved

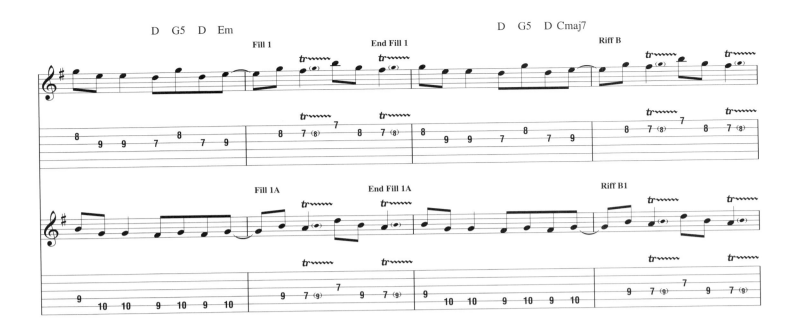

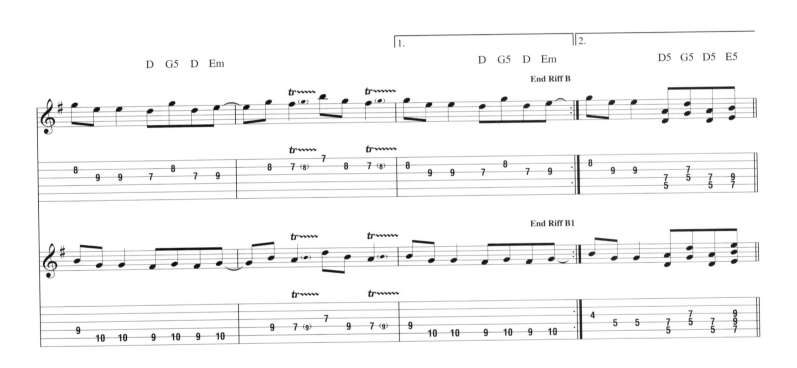

Verse

2nd & 3rd times, Gtrs. 1 & 2: w/ Rhy. Fig. 1 (1 1/3 times)

1. You'll take my life but I'll take yours too. ___
2. The horse, he sweats with fear; we break to run. ___
3. We got so close, near e - nough to fight. ___

You'll fire your mus - ket but I'll
The might - y roar of the
When a Rus - sian gets me

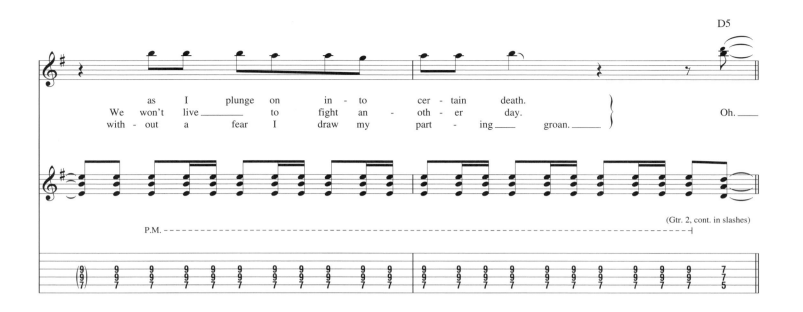

as I plunge on in - to cer - tain death.
We won't live_____ to fight an - oth - er day.
with - out a fear I draw my part - ing_____ groan._____

Oh._____

Chorus

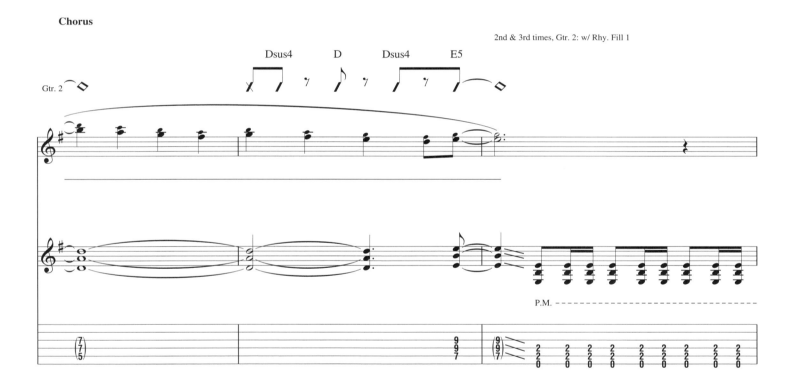

2nd & 3rd times, Gtr. 2: w/ Rhy. Fill 1

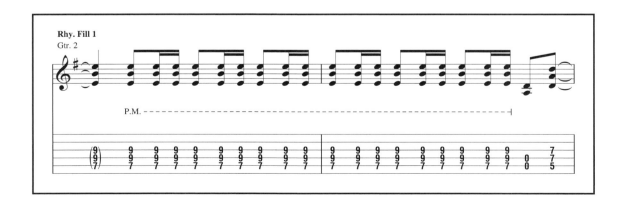

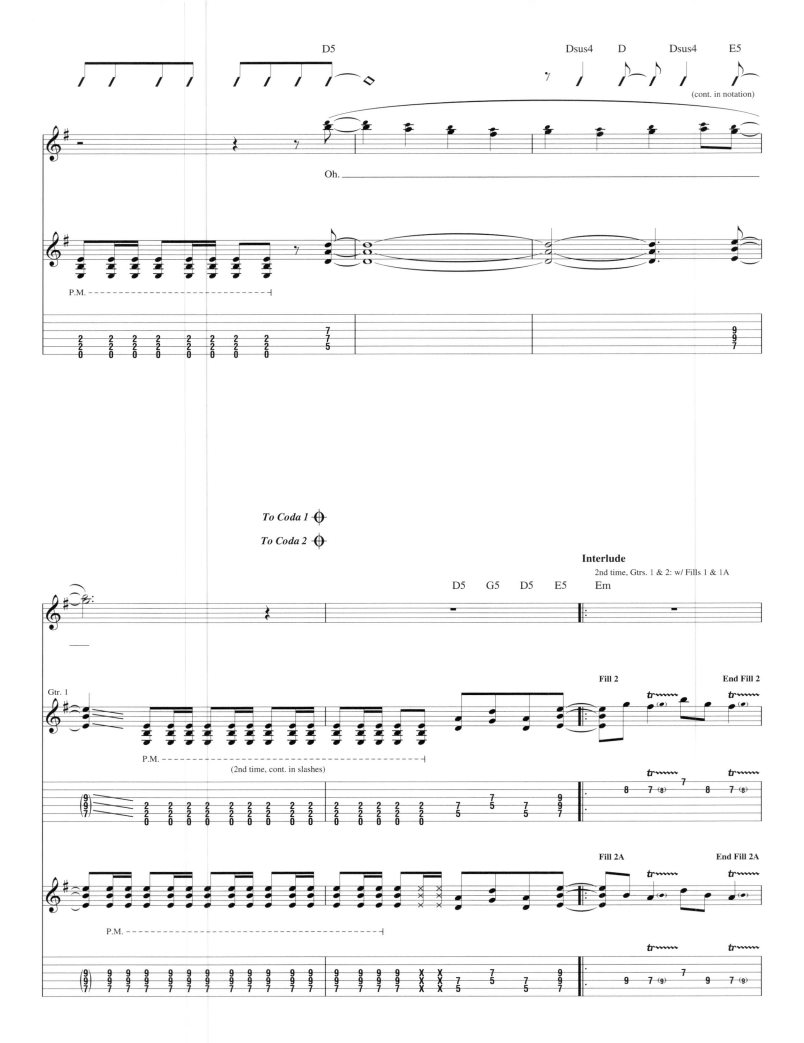

Gtrs. 1 & 2: w/ Riffs B & B1 (last 3 meas.)   Gtrs. 1 & 2: w/ Riffs B & B1 (1st meas.)

D G5 D Em   D G5 D Cmaj7

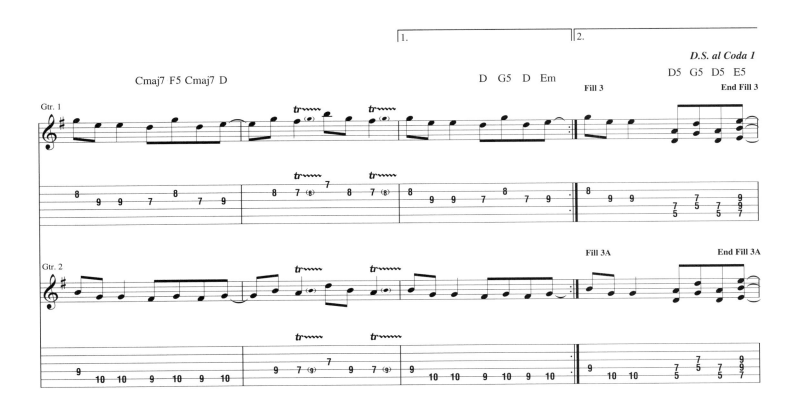

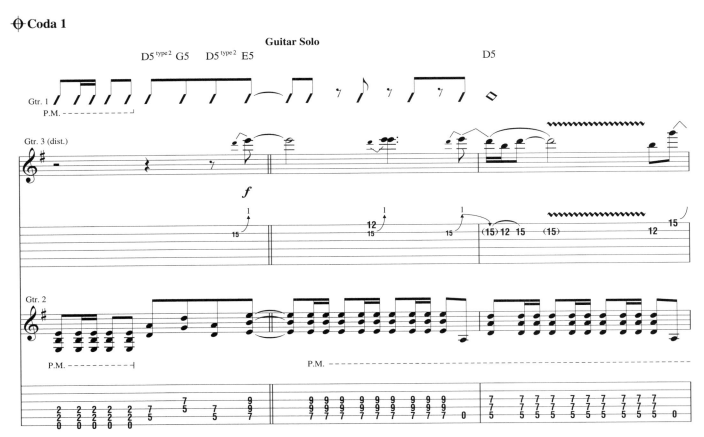

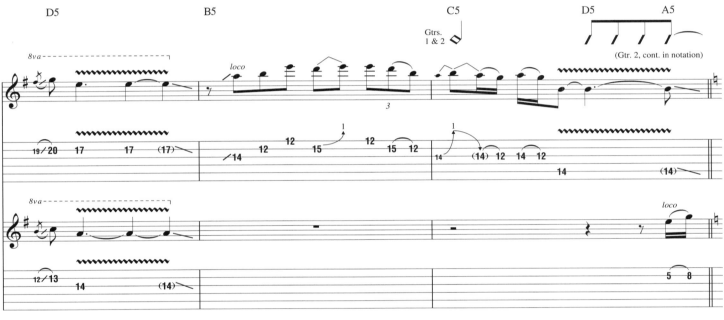

Guitar Solo

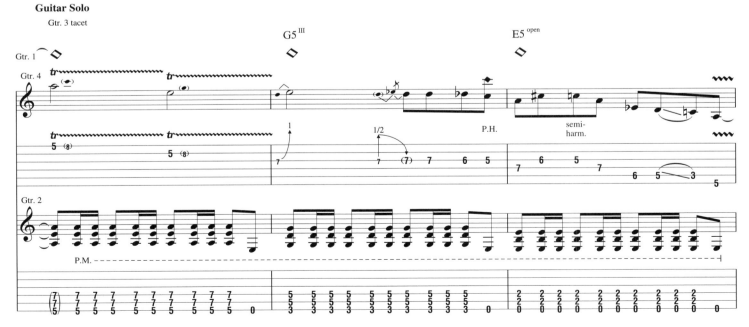

157

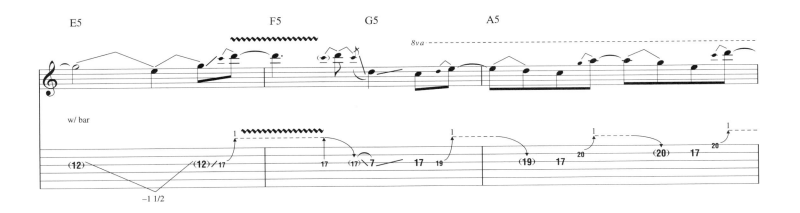

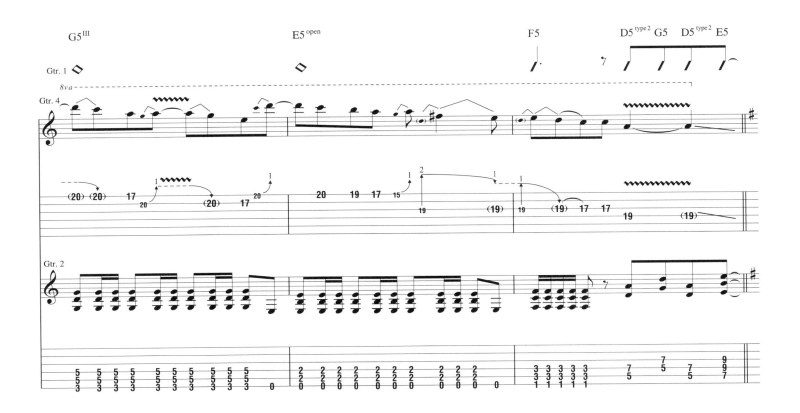

Interlude

1st time, Gtrs. 1 & 2: w/ Fills 2 & 2A
1st time, Gtr. 4 tacet
2nd time, Gtrs. 1 & 2: w/ Fills 1 & 1A

Gtrs. 1 & 2: w/ Riffs B & B1 (last 3 meas.)

Em   **D G5 D Em**   **D G5 D Cmaj7**

1st time, Gtrs. 1 & 2: w/ Riffs B & B1
2nd time, Gtrs. 1 & 2: w/ Riffs B & B1 (1st 3 meas.)

| 1. | | 2. |

D.S. al Coda 2

Gtrs. 1 & 2: w/ Fills 3 & 3A

D G5 D D6sus²⁄₄   **D G5 D Em**   **D G5 D E5**

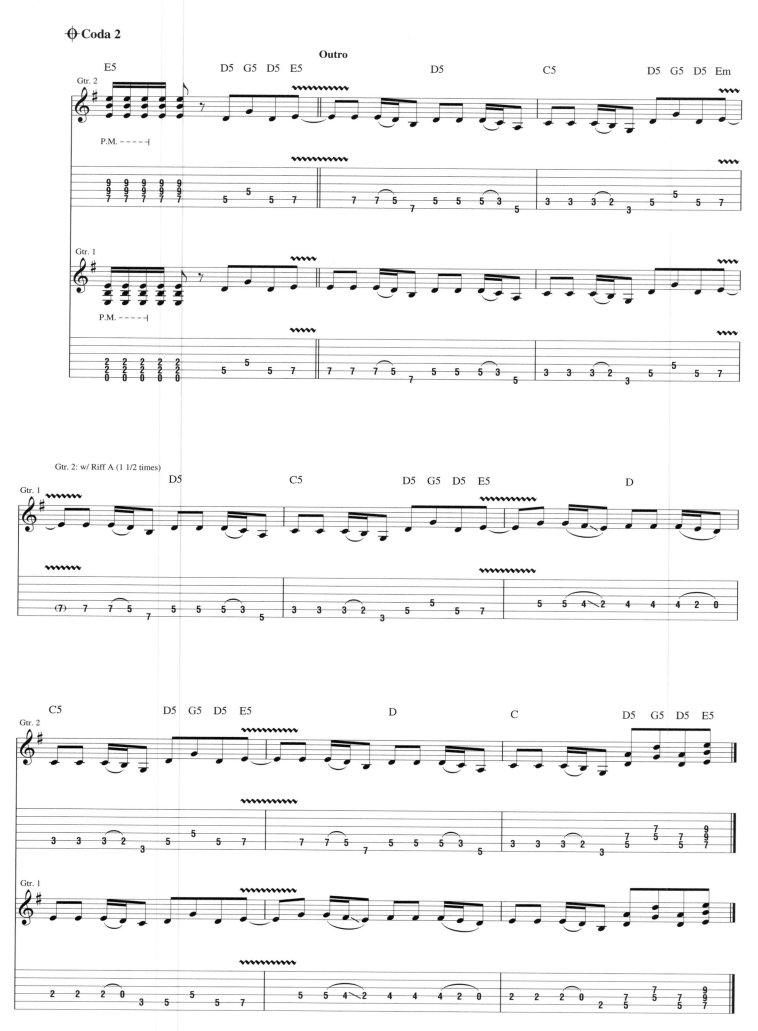

from *Powerslave*

Two Minutes to Midnight

Words and Music by Bruce Dickinson and Adrian Smith

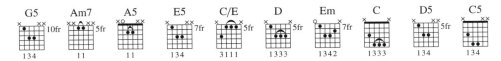

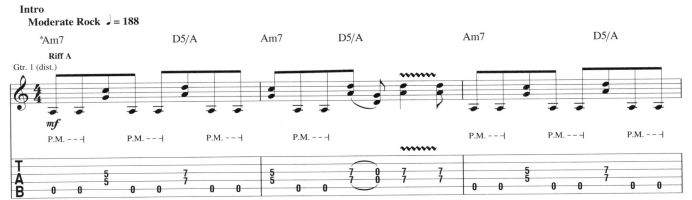

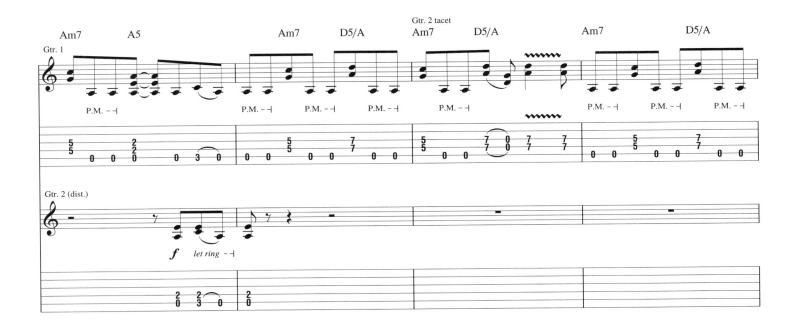

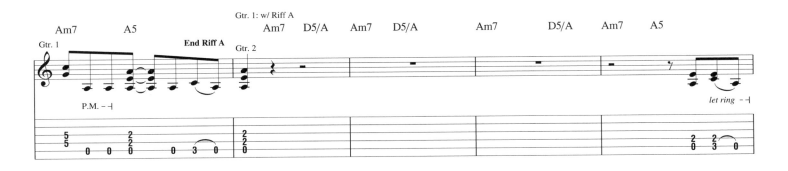

Copyright © 1984 by Iron Maiden Holdings Ltd.
All Rights in the world Administered by Zomba Music Publishers Ltd.
All Rights in the United States and Canada Administered by Zomba Enterprises, Inc.
International Copyright Secured   All Rights Reserved

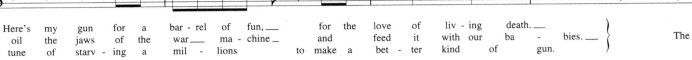
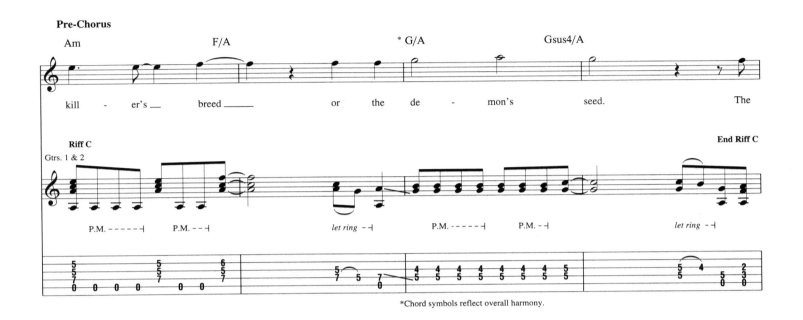
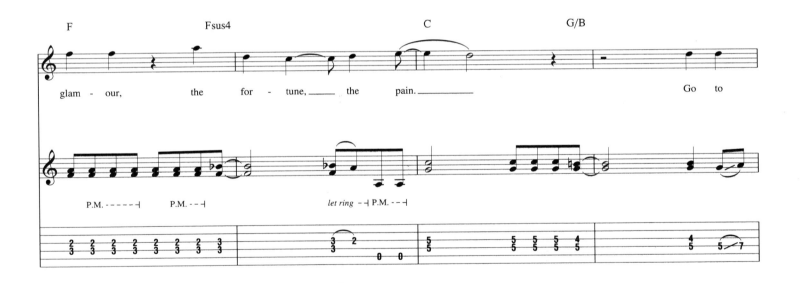

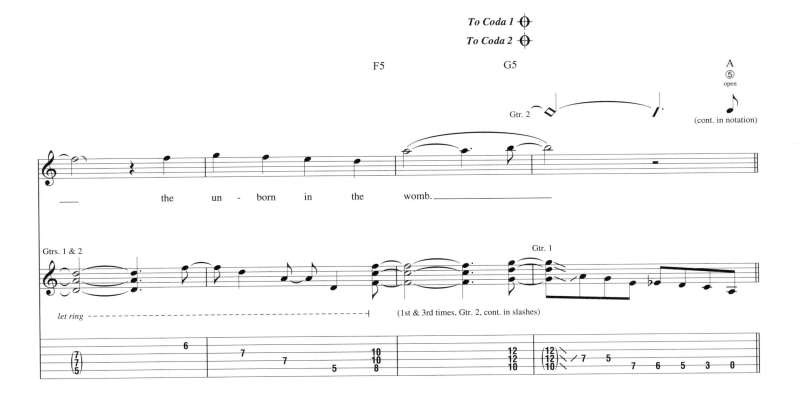

Interlude

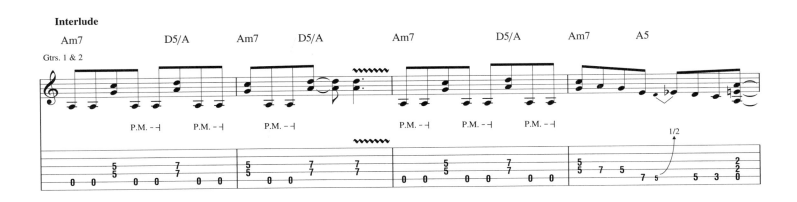

D.S. al Coda 1

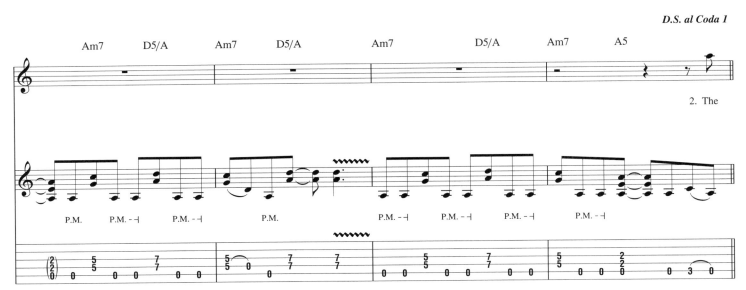

2. The

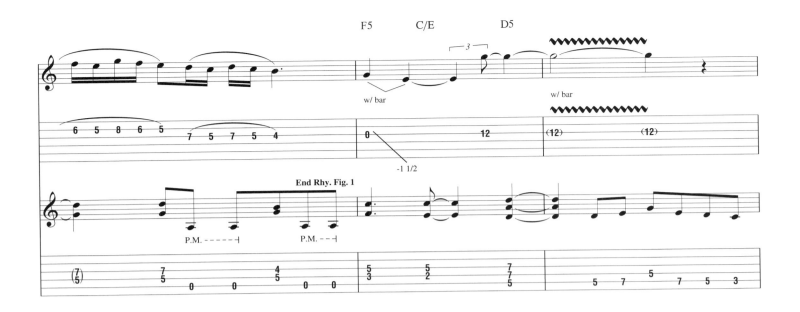

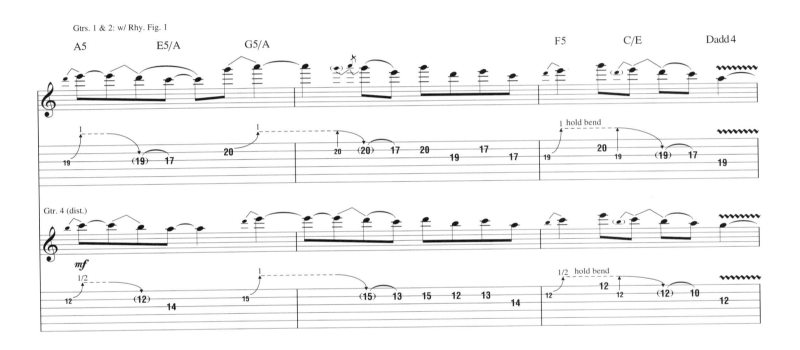

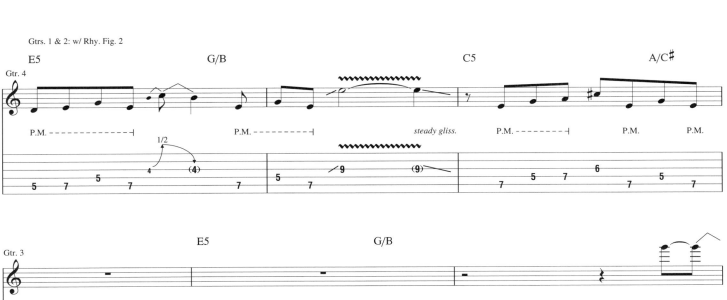

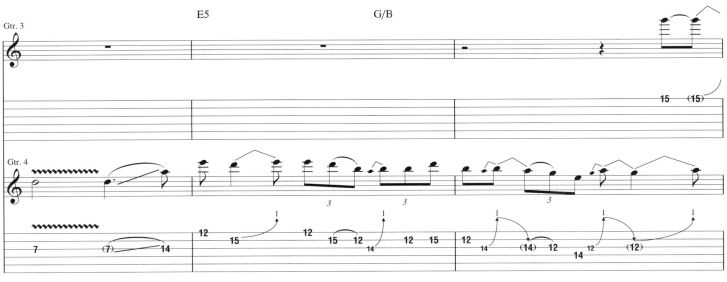

Interlude

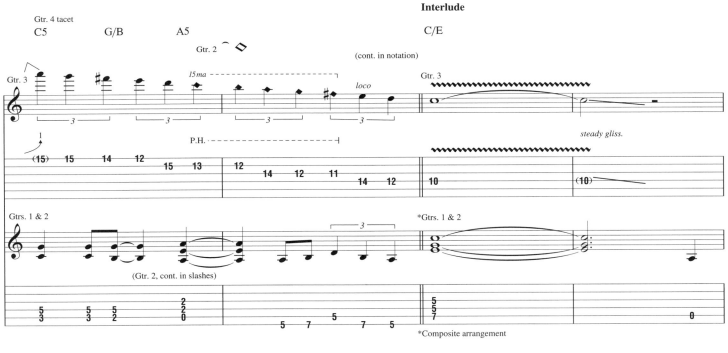

*Composite arrangement

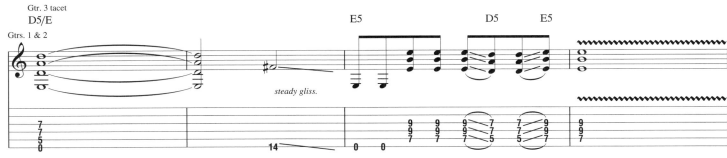

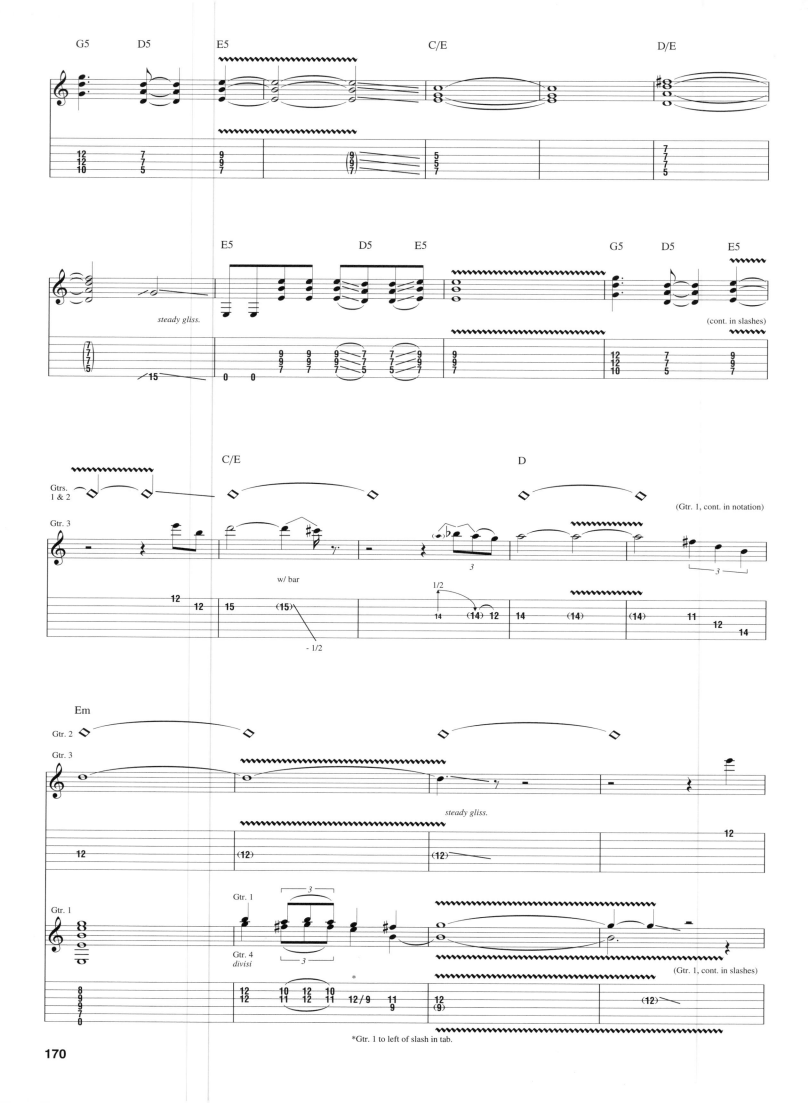

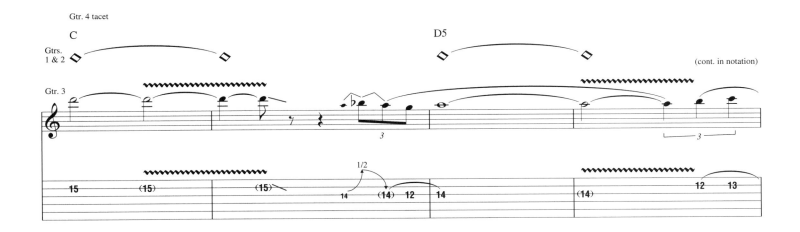

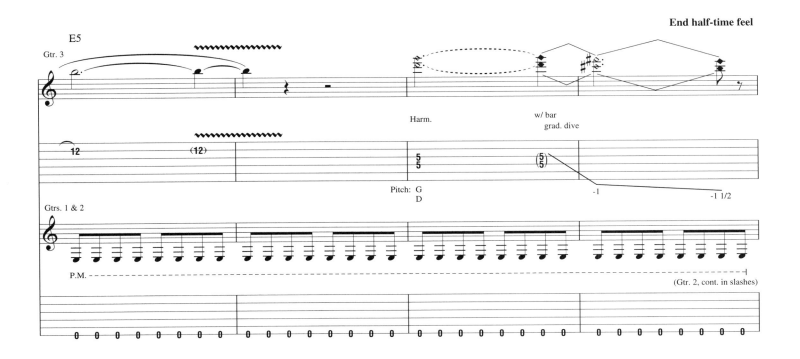

End half-time feel

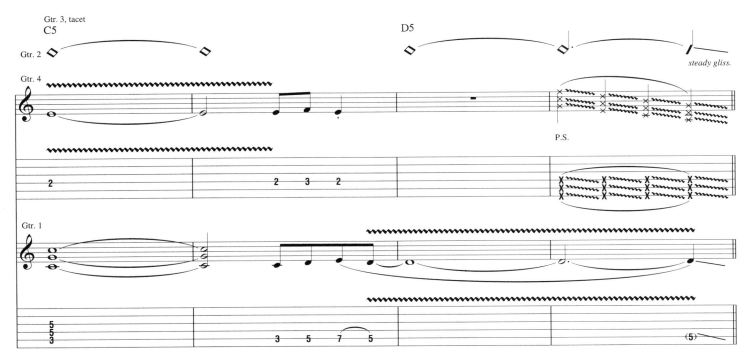

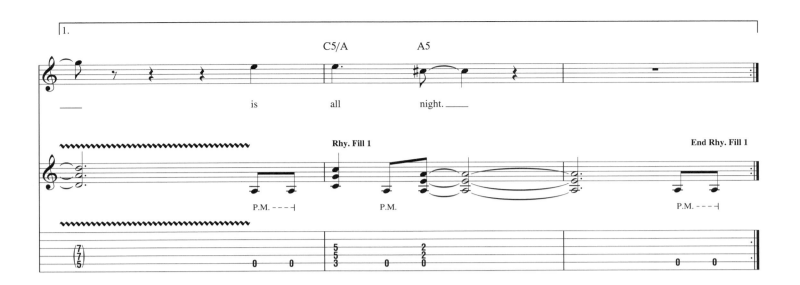

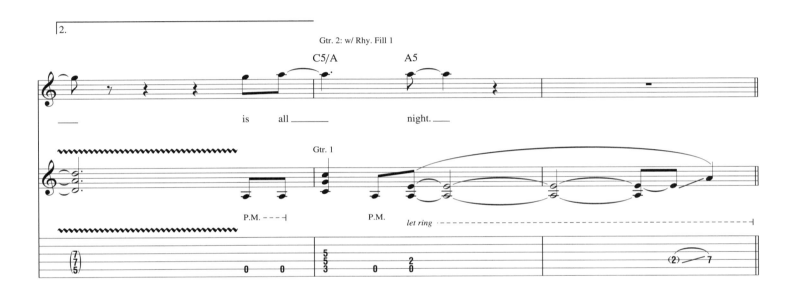

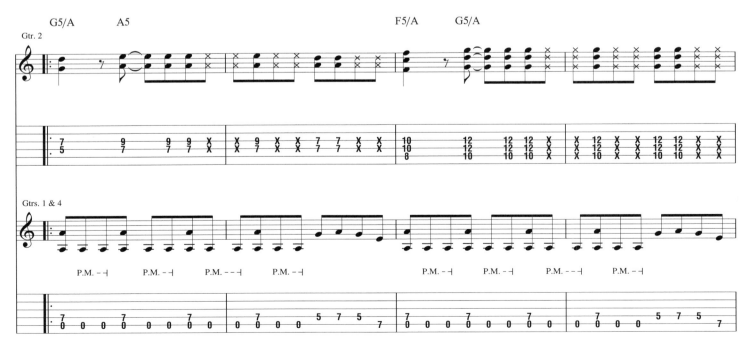

from *Somewhere in Time*
Wasted Years
Words and Music by Adrian Smith

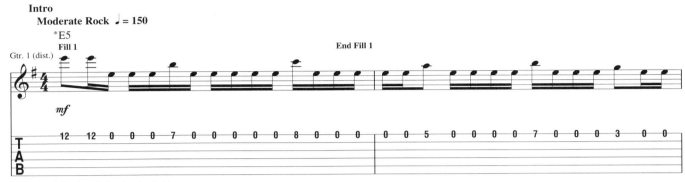

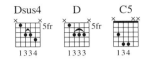

*Chord symbols reflect implied harmony.

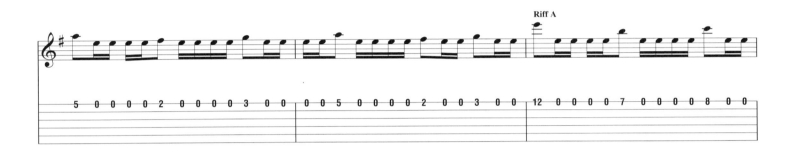

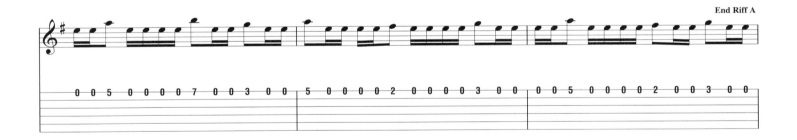

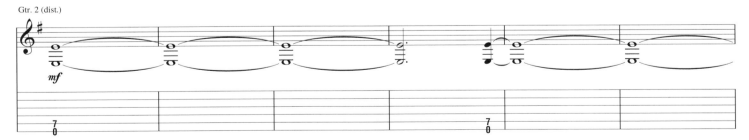

Copyright © 1986 by Iron Maiden Holdings Ltd.
All Rights in the world Administered by Zomba Music Publishers Ltd.
All Rights in the United States and Canada Administered by Zomba Enterprises, Inc.
International Copyright Secured   All Rights Reserved

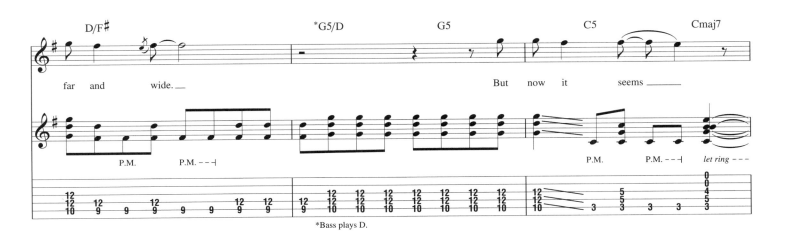

*Bass plays D.

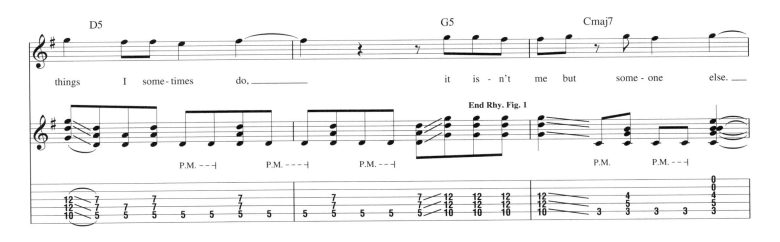

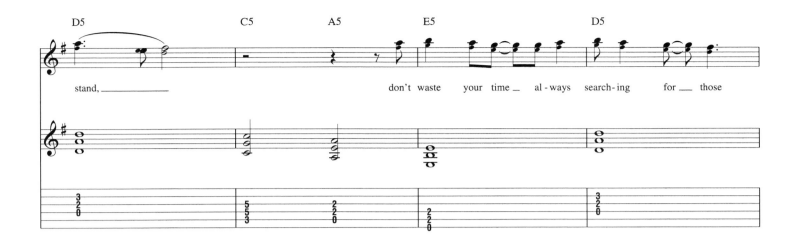

don't waste your time al-ways search-ing for those

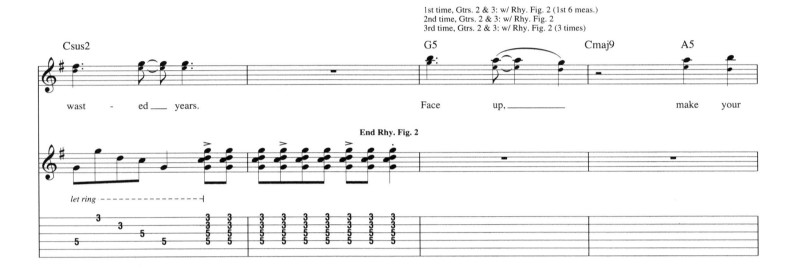

wast - ed years. Face up, make your

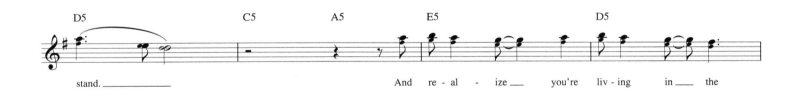

stand. And re-al - ize you're liv-ing in the

To Coda ⊕
Interlude

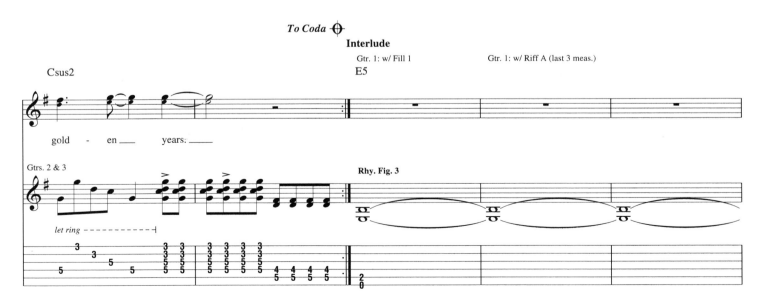

gold - en years.

179

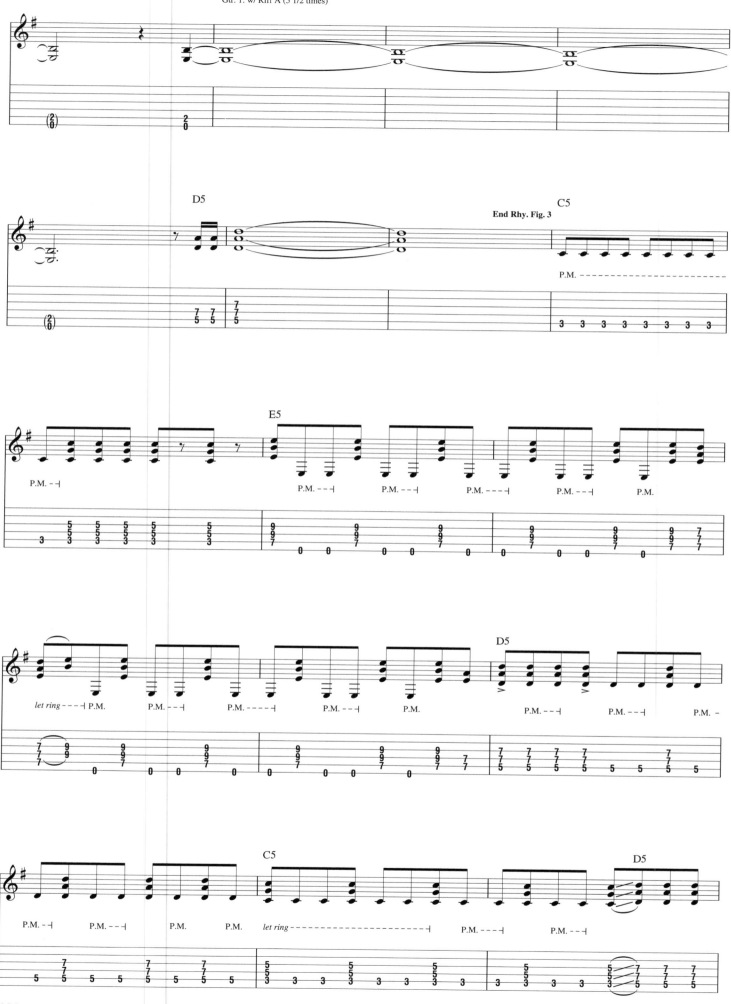

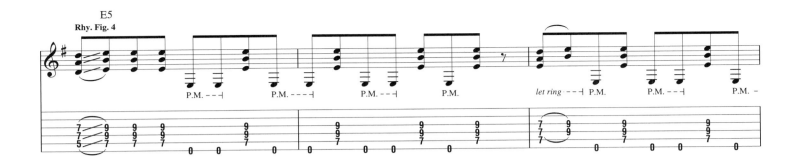

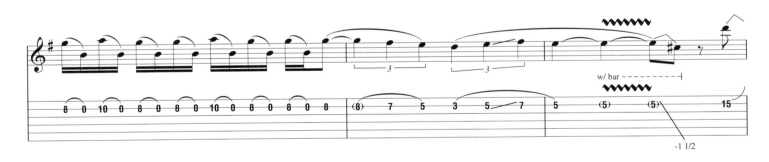

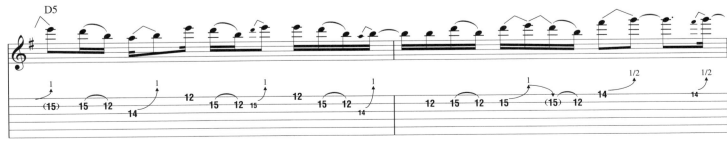

182

from *Killers*

Wrathchild

Words and Music by Steven Harris

Copyright © 1980 by Iron Maiden Holdings Ltd.
All Rights in the world Administered by Zomba Music Publishers Ltd.
All Rights in the United States and Canada Administered by Zomba Enterprises, Inc.
International Copyright Secured   All Rights Reserved

Interlude

*Gtrs. 2 & 3

*Gtr. 3 w/ slight P.M. (next 8 meas.).

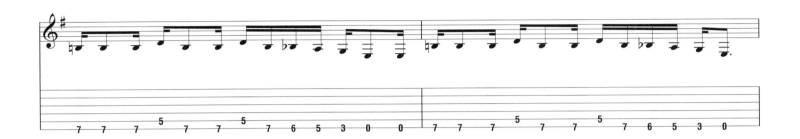

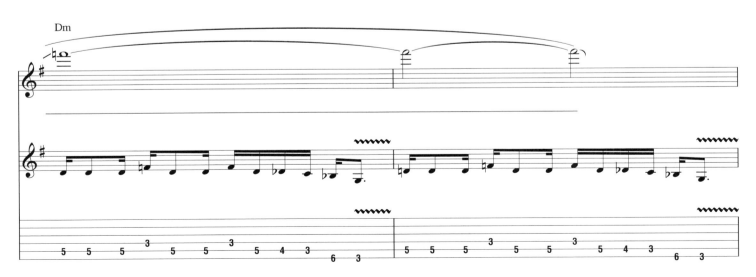

189

Guitar Solo

Gtr. 2: w/ Rhy. Fig. 1 (2 times)
Gtr. 3: w/ Rhy. Fig. 3 (2 times)

Verse

Gtrs. 2 & 3: w/ Rhy. Fig. 1 (2 times)
Gtr. 4 tacet

2. Say it does-n't mat-ter, ain't noth-ing gon-na al-ter the cours-es of my des-ti-na-tion. I

know I've got-ta find___ se-ri-ous peace of mind or I know I'll just___ go cra-zy.___

Pre-Chorus

Gtrs. 2 & 3: w/ Rhy. Fig. 2

Now I spend___ my time___ look-ing all a-round___

Gtr. 4

for a man that's no - where to be found. ____ Yeah. Un - til I find __ him, I'm

Gtr. 4 tacet

nev - er gon - na stop search - ing. I'm go - ing to find __ my man, __   gon - na

Gtr. 2: w/ Rhy. Fig. 1 (2 times)
Gtr. 3: w/ Rhy. Fig. 3 (2 times)

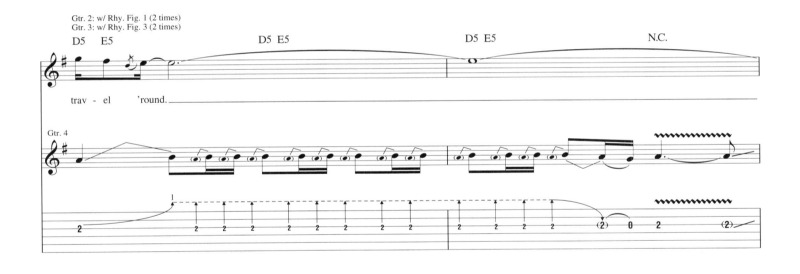

trav - el 'round. ____

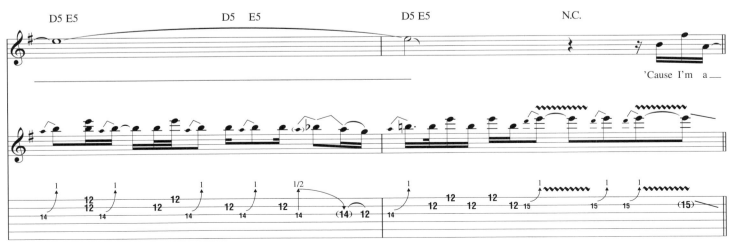

'Cause I'm a __